CHOSEN

A Memoir

by **Elizabeth Jane Pryce**

With Thanks

Jane ☺

Chosen

ISBN:978-1-7341878-3-0

Book Design by Jill Flores
Author photo by David W. Wakeling
All other photographs from Elizabeth Jane Pryce's private albums.

Published by Independent Writers Studio Press
Bellingham, Washington

First Printing Edition

This book is dedicated to my dear friend
Sally Lee Hansberry, who passed away on 21st July 2021.
You are sorely missed. I just couldn't write fast enough.
I will always be grateful for your comments
and edits on the stories you read.

ACKNOWLEDGEMENTS

I would like to thank all my wonderful first readers, editors, and proof-readers, Jennifer Woods, Rita Saling, Natasha Tolley, Harold Hansberry, Callum McSherry, Mary Gillilan, and Dana Lyon Edward, for all the hours of reading and their positive and helpful comments.

Also, I'd like to thank my fellow writers in the Blue Bottles Writing Studio and Mary Gillilan's Independent Writers Studio for their support and encouragement.

Last but not least, I'd like to thank Jill Flores, the graphic designer, once again, for her persistence and careful editing as well as her patience and professional approach.

ABOUT THE AUTHOR

Elizabeth Jane Pryce was born in the seaside town of Bridport, Dorset, England, in 1949. At the tender age of six months, Jane's grandmother came to England, taking her back to the island of Barbados in the Caribbean to raise her as her child. After fourteen years, Elizabeth Jane left her island home for England, believing she would return within a year.

Once in England, the cast and setting of her life suddenly changed. To survive emotionally, she lived a double life, an internal one of sadness, missing her "Mummy and Daddy," and an external life crammed with as much activity as possible.

Elizabeth married in 1972, raised three children, and moved to Bellingham in 1991 after her divorce. A passionate gardener, she became a landscaper and began writing.

She is the author of *Wild Child* (2010), a collection of poems about the influences of her early life. Her poetry has appeared in *Clover, A Literary Rag*, and a poem in *Borders: An Anthology of Stories*. She is one of four independent authors who published *The Blue Bottles Writing Studio: A Variety of Stories* as part of a writers group she still organizes and runs.

Elizabeth devotes herself to her garden and the Blue Bottles writer group. She is at work on her second memoir, which takes the reader to England after Elizabeth's return from her island home at the age of fourteen.

PROLOGUE

My grandparents, my "Mummy and Daddy," were both born in England at the end of the nineteenth century. My grandfather was first-generation English, descended from a long line of people from the Netherlands. He was born into a family of seven children and raised in strict Plymouth Brethren style. My grandmother's heritage was Welsh and English. She was born into a family of six and raised in the Protestant religion. They both descended from headstrong and determined families.

They both grew up at the height of colonialism when the British Empire dominated over a quarter of the earth's land surface. My grandmother had a more polite approach to other races of people, but my grandfather demanded the respect he felt entitled to as a White British man.

My grandparents raised their first family, including my mother, the youngest of four children, in New South Wales, Australia. They had a farm and freedom and were both hard workers, but it was a precarious life at best. They were living on the outskirts of society, in a hard-scrabble for survival. My grandparents cut the trees and pulled the stumps before they could till the land. The home for the two adults and four children was a one-room galvanized shack with sheets hung over the beams as dividers for privacy. Rabbits disturbed the well-swept dirt floors at night, often appearing under the beds.

When they moved their young family to St. Vincent in the Caribbean in the early 1930s, they never returned to Australia. The oldest three children left for England at different points during the Second World War. After the war their son, Douglas, returned and stayed in Barbados, Lorna and Anne remained in England. The youngest daughter, Thea, left the islands for England in 1948 to visit her sisters without explaining that she was pregnant. The following year Mummy went to England and brought the baby back to Barbados. I was that baby, and this is my story of my fourteen years growing up in the Caribbean.

BARBADOS

1950–1956

Early Years

According to my birth mother whom I didn't know until I was a young and immature teenager — I was conceived out of wedlock from a date rape in Barbados and born in a back room of a house in Bridport, England.

My grandmother came to England from the Caribbean on the pretence of being lonely and wanting to visit her daughters. She planned to adopt me without telling her husband I was his youngest daughter's child. My grandmother wanted to protect my mother and me from scandal. When my grandmother left England and took me back to Barbados, I was eleven months of age. I wouldn't hear from my mother again until I was over fourteen years old.

My grandmother and I flew BOAC, (British Overseas Airways Corporation, a predecessor of British Airways) from London to Barbados with a stopover in Nassau, Bahamas. I was now my grandmother's daughter and would grow up calling her and my grandfather, Mummy and Daddy.

I slept most of the way to Nassau, even swallowing in my sleep to relieve ear pressure caused by the rapid air changes as the plane took off and landed.

"You've a natural flyer there, ma'am," the air hostess told Mummy, who loved to retell stories about bringing me home.

From all the letters written to her daughters, and sisters to sisters, and stories told by Mummy, I was a very happy child; I took everything in *my stride and was as fit as a fiddle*, one letter reported. I loved the story about our stopover in Nassau: how I danced on her feet and banged the side of the bathtub when I saw it, shouting "Ba, ba, ba," frantically trying to tear off my clothes. According to Mummy, the bath was my joy. *She can plug up the bath & have a swim, or 'wim,' as she says.* She also told me the story of how I loved my first taste of paw-paw or papaya, and how excited I was later, seeing a similarly coloured food on Mummy's plate, followed by my disgust when it wasn't — it was pumpkin. "If looks could kill," she'd say with a laugh.

Once we arrived in Barbados, I ran around the house as though I had always lived there, took the hands of both of my grandparents *as if it was the most natural thing to do*. It took me a couple of weeks to make friends with the dogs and cats. I would come to love all animals, even the chickens, whom I loved to arrange and rearrange on their roosts before allowing them to go to sleep. In a couple of years, I would have my own dog that I called Pedro, a half boxer, half Labrador, with whom I would roll around on the floor sharing a bone!

In a letter, Mummy reported that I was *simply crazy over planes*, especially the BOAC ones, calling them *Lorna's planes*. (Lorna was Mummy's first child.) I kept asking when she was coming to visit. I was already showing signs of being left-handed at a year and a half, *automatically stepping off with her left foot and feed*(ing) *herself also with her left hand*, Mummy wrote to Lorna. She also wrote, *her sense of humour, mischief, and fun are highly developed* and Daddy was completely captivated by me, calling me a good *little trooper*. He apparently gave me a dancing lesson one day and I was so excited that I continued to dance in the bath, splashing water everywhere much to Mummy's chagrin.

My first vivid memory in Barbados was of a baby doll I received for my second Christmas. I opened my eyes and looked up into the face of an exquisite toy. "My baby, my baby, I want my baby," I kept saying until Mummy lifted me from under the mosquito net and gave me the doll. I spent the rest of the day walking around rocking "my baby" in my arms. It was a beautiful celluloid doll with moulded hair and rosy cheeks. It had eyes that opened and shut and was dressed in a long white lacy voile gown and bonnet.

I have another memory of a birthday picnic, probably my second birthday, with Mummy and Daddy, their son Douglas, his wife, and my three cousins; it was from a boot of a car on the beach. Mummy's good friend, Garth Dean, was also there. I remember, of all things, my cousin Dorn, who was a few months younger than me. While he stood on a box peeing into the back of the toilet, I sat on the front of the seat supported by their Black mammy; she took care of Dorn and me when Mummy was busy.

We lived in so many different houses, it is hard to place memories with the right house, but we lived in one home built on stilts, right on the beach. While we lived in this house, I became sick with a nasty bout of whooping cough. I was confined to the house for six months. I remember that it was horrible being sick. I threw up almost every day, once so violently that the bowl I carried fell out of my hands and broke. It was a favourite of mine; bunnies ran around the rim. It had encouraged me to eat my breakfast every morning.

"Eat your porridge before the bunnies tuck in; they are fat enough already," Mummy would say with a smile.

Every morning Mummy gave me a large tablespoon of cod liver oil followed by a treat, a tablespoon of thick, brown, caramel-like malt called Virol. It always went down very nicely, but after a while, it tasted awful. I was tired of being sick and complained, saying, "I wish I were dead."

"Don't say that," Mummy said. "When I was a little girl, I had whooping cough for almost a year. I also had scarlet fever and diphtheria. I was continuously sick until I was about twelve. But my baby sister, Adelaide, died from scarlet fever. It was the saddest and most terrible time of my life. Addie was only six-years-old. I never want to hear you wish for death again."

The best part of the ordeal was walking along the beach with Daddy in the evenings when there was no one else around. It felt wonderful to play in the warm cream-coloured sand. That was when Daddy taught me to float in the sea.

Mummy was never a fancy cook. She believed in simple healthy food. But like most other things in her life, she put magic in her fingers when she made food for me. To persuade me to eat pumpkin, she called them yellow potatoes, or mixed with bananas, it became golden sweet fritters. Spinach, a dark green homogenous bulk sitting on my plate, eventually became magic too. Mummy told me the stories of Popeye the Sailor Man; I believed I could also be invincible! The Christmas of my recovery, we received a Christmas package from relatives in America containing cans of blueberries, with which Mummy made a pie. I knew I was getting better because the taste of those blueberries equalled nothing I had eaten before or since. We also received Thompson raisins, as big as quarters, and with a distinct flavour and sweetness; I can still taste them in my dreams.

While Daddy stayed at home dreaming up schemes and projects for his farming ideas, Mummy worked as a bookkeeper for the largest hotel on the island, the Coral Reef Hotel. I often went with her to avoid being under Daddy's feet, and I loved riding on the back of Mummy's bicycle. On the way to Mummy's work, we'd stop to feed the monkey, which was in a cage built into the wall beneath the owner's house.

I loved walking around the hotel; it was exotic. I loved the dining room in the mornings, the sunbeams streaming through the glass. I loved the polished mahogany tables, the crisp Irish linen tablecloths, napkins, and the white china with small golden rolls of butter waiting to go on white bread, warm from the oven. Sometimes, I would eat breakfast at the hotel if there weren't too many guests staying at the time. I loved to put the Robinson Golden Shred Marmalade on the white crusty bread rolls, which we never had at home. I could have a whole glass of fresh milk, too, if I wanted.

The large glass windows of the hotel dining room looked out over the immaculate gardens winding through the mahogany, frangipani, and flamboyant trees, stretching down to the gentle blue lapping waters of the Atlantic Ocean. I loved watching the hummingbirds and the yellow winged bananaquits, or sugarbirds as the locals called them. They flitted through the gardens, sipping honey from the scented flowers. Sometimes the sugarbirds, seeing the dishes of golden butter, would crash into the glass windows in their desire to reach the food. I was always sad when this happened because they either broke their necks or died from the shock of hitting the glass.

In the hotel basement, there were large fish tanks that ran the length of the wall on the ocean side of the hotel. Huge pipes buried under the sand connected the tanks with the Atlantic. I spent many wonderful afternoons with the scientist who worked there. He was studying marine life, especially that of green sea turtles. All kinds of exotic creatures came in through the pipes. Once, I was lucky enough to see a couple of tiny exquisite seahorses; it was a fascinating time.

It was probably the first time I ate turtle eggs. They were round like a ping-pong ball, but soft and squishy without much taste. Mummy, Daddy, and I had more fun tossing them around the kitchen at home than eating them.

We also had guinea fowl, chickens, and turkeys in one of our homes in Barbados. I loved the brown chicken eggs with their bright orange yolks, but the guinea fowl I only remember as extremely noisy. The birds immediately raised the alarm with piercing screeches and cackles, whenever someone approached the house.

"Better than a guard dog," Mummy said.

I was about three and a half when my big sister, Anne, was married; I was her flower girl. Writing to Lorna about Anne's wedding, Mummy wrote that I handled Anne's bouquet *without fuss and all unrehearsed. She wore a white voile frock, smocked with the colours of her hat trimmed on the brim with shells dyed and sewn on like flowers. She really looked lovely, Jane was as good as gold, and all the old aunts and uncles just went crazy over her.*

Mummy wrote to Lorna, *I can truthfully tell you he* (Daddy) *has done far more for me and Jane than ever he did when you all were kiddies. As you see it pays to have a second childhood.*

But there was one occasion when Daddy frightened me. He tripped over an object I left on the living room floor and he shouted at me. I ran outside and crawled up under the house, refusing to come out. Daddy's angry voice terrified me. I stayed under the house, even though Daddy tried to persuade me to come out, until Mummy came home from the hotel. She talked me out of my cramped place in a matter-of-fact way, which I trusted; Mummy never had emotional outbursts.

"You must be hungry, and your little legs must be stiff by now."

"Daddy's going to spank me," I said with a hiccup in my voice.

"Daddy's not angry now. He wants you to come out from under the house and come inside. Will you come out now?"

"Will you hold my hand, please, Mummy?"

"I will if you get yourself over to where I am, then I'll hold your hand and we can go inside together. After supper, you can tell Daddy you're sorry for what you did."

"Yes, Mummy," I said sadly.

"You're a silly goose to be afraid of Daddy; his bark is worse than his bite."

I knew she was right; she was always right.

When I crawled out, all she said was, "Right, childie, into the shower with you, wash off those cobwebs, and I'll have dinner ready in two shakes of a lamb's tail."

Later, when I was ready for bed, I went to say goodnight to Daddy.

"Just be more careful with your things Janie, we don't need anyone having an accident around here." He hugged and kissed me goodnight.

The discovery of letters from my grandmother (Mummy) to her daughters when I was a small child has greatly impacted my emotional well-being. *I am so excited over it all that I am always bubbling over, it's more than 'fantastic.'* But I also find it troubling how flippant she could be. *I can manage to wangle Daddy because he knows I have always wanted to adopt another child or two. In a way I wish I could bring two out, it would confuse the issue wouldn't it?*

As for Jane, she is delightful, so pretty, lovable, strong, straight, and above all brainy that I think there will be not much expense where her schooling is concerned, for she should win all the scholarships she needs. Even as a tiny child she show(s) reasoning power, of no mean quality. Also, she is thorough in anything she does, if it is done one way to-day, it must be the same weeks ahead. Not too bad as to clearing up her toys, though she has not many now. Pedro (our dog) has chewed up two or three tiny dolls. But she seems to keep happy and busy most of the time.

Dad made her a duck rocker for Xmas and that keeps her going a bit, then the canna seed pods and bougainvillea, stones, and shells that she picks up all serve their purpose. A tablespoon of flour, when I am baking, in the bakelite cups she has, serves as food for the doll, and it's lovely to see her put a feeder (bib) on before she starts.

Though she lets others kiss her, so far the dolls & I am the only ones she kisses, quite a victory on my part. She nearly emptied a tube of ointment on (the) centre table & her hair, plus some brilliantine & shaving cream all in one day. Have shampooed her hair twice under shower 2-3 times per day & I still cannot get it all out. Dad is still as crazy as I am over her.

Captain Tom and the Hurricaine

Our next home was a big stone colonial house. We lived there for a year while the vicar, his wife, and their daughter were away; living there was unique. Their daughter had all kinds of exciting toys, like a 'real' iron and a doll that walked and said, "Mama" when I turned her over. This doll had soft curly hair and cute little girl dresses. I called her Harriet while she was mine. The grounds were spacious and ran down to the sea and sandy beaches. There was an old wooden seesaw on the grounds. It was built using a split tree as a central base. I loved to go on it when someone was around to push me up and down. It was here that I started school at the tender age of four.

My teacher, Captain Tom, was a retired sea captain who lived in a small cottage on the grounds. He was a gruff-looking man with large bushy sideburns and a loud resonating voice. He wore a peaked hat with a large embroidered gold anchor on the front, which he perched on the front of his desk while teaching. I was the youngest of ten or twelve children of varying ages. The small classroom had three or four bench seats with sloping desktops made of polished wood which sat on a raised platform, about a foot off the floor.

Daddy made a small box for me to place on the bench because my eyes barely came over the top. I have a strong memory of using a small wooden framed blackboard to write letters and numbers and a colourful abacus. The bright yellow, red, and orange beads were smooth and pretty. I enjoyed counting. I could already read simple stories.

❧ ⚬ ◈ ⚬ ❧

Hurricane Janet* struck in September 1955, just before I turned six. It was one of the most powerful Atlantic hurricanes since 1780. While the hurricane raged and ravaged the island, I played with the dolls in the old colonial nursery. Memory is a funny thing — even the most significant events in our lives can read like a fantasy when related to others. I was only five years old, yet I remember standing alone watching the wind in the trees from the nursery window and hearing the roar of the distant ocean.

I recall walking with Captain Tom, my small hand in his large one, after the hurricane; the "big winds," as the natives called it, had abated. I was awed and saddened by the devastation of the gardens and the broken and battered trees.

"Oh! My seesaw is gone. Why are all the trees broken?" I asked, looking up at the Captain.

"Because of the hurricane, of course!" He shouted in my ear. His loud voice frightened me and I tried to pull my hand away, but Captain Tom held on tightly. I felt I should have known better than to ask because of how he spoke. I didn't say anything else, even when I saw that the sandy beach was gone. Broken trees and debris now covered the creamy white sand. The foaming waves, like gigantic seahorses, were coming up through the trees. There was nowhere to build sandcastles with Daddy or show him how well I could float.

Above the ocean's roar, I heard another sound, loud and booming. Explosions of water were flying high above the natural breakers as they crashed against the rocks and shore. Captain Tom began to shout angrily and waved his cane in the air at a group of Black men, who looked like they were standing on the ocean waves.

The captain's rage made me even more afraid. I tried to pull my hand away again, but he shouted at me to be still, then abruptly dropped my hand and ran to the foaming edge of the water, yelling at the men. "Stop that! Get the hell out of the sea! God will punish your wickedness. I am calling the police."

I stood terrified at the edge of the trees, trying to avoid getting my feet wet, while the captain waded in up to his knees, striking out at the men as they came in on the waves and took off. The captain stormed back to the house with me running tearfully behind him, trying to keep up. He seemed to have forgotten all about me. While Daddy called the police, Mummy made tea.

I don't remember if the police caught the men, but I do remember

10

being afraid to come into the living room when the police arrived at the house later. They came to discuss the incident with Captain Tom. I was upset by the policemen talking loudly.

Blast fishing**, which the Black men were doing, used explosives to stun or kill schools of fish for collection. It was illegal to catch and sell fish in this way because it left traces of poison, making people sick.

One year later, we moved to Monserrat taking only essentials; we left my pets behind.

Footnote:
* Hurricane Janet hit the island of Barbados on September 22nd 1955, becoming one of the most powerful Atlantic hurricanes on record since the Great Hurricane of 1780.
** Blast fishing, a practice of using a Molotov cocktail to stun or kill schools of fish for collection, was illegal and destructive to the surrounding ecosystem.

Jane, 6th months old

Jane with
Anne and Pedro

Jane with Anne

Flower girl at Anne's wedding

Coral Reef
Hotel

Jane with Dorn

MONSERRAT

1956–1958

Monserrat

I remember nothing of our leaving Barbados. I believe I was traumatised by the loss of everything I was leaving behind: my cousins, my school playmates, Pedro, my dog, Moony, my cat, and the wonderful Coral Reef Hotel. But Daddy was so excited about the prospects of working for the government that we were naturally happy too; he was going to teach the farmers to grow tomatoes and sea island cotton.

We moved into a single-story old wooden house built on an embankment above the main road that came up from Plymouth. The property had a large hollow tree on one side and a gnarled tamarind tree on the other side. Mrs. Shand, an ample-girthed lady whose face always lit up with a friendly smile when she saw us, lived across the road. She became Mummy's best friend. They remained friends long after we left the island.

On the hollow tree side of our house, there was a row of grand brick homes. They had a private tennis court and swimming pool, which outsiders were barred from using. The people who lived there were part of a tight-knit community Mummy referred to as "hoity-toity." I sometimes saw the lady who lived in the first house on the row. She had sharp, angular features and pitch-black hair and lived alone with two cats.

At the back of our house was scrubland stretching to a point where I could just see the roof of the nearest building; the property of a lady called Monica. She was my idea of a princess! Monica wore beautiful soft, flowing dresses, which she wore to cover her thin unused legs. Monica didn't walk; I believe she had survived polio. Mummy referred to her as "being delicate." Monica spent all her time either lying in a lacy hammock or sitting in her studio, painting. She painted stained glass windows, one of which hung in the church in Plymouth. I liked the lovely, older woman who may have been Monica's mother, who lived in with the family because she made lovely afternoon tea and cakes whenever I visited the boys: Graham and Thomas.

17

I started school almost immediately once we arrived on the island of Montserrat, at an Anglican Convent for girls. The nuns were strict but fair. They wore brown habits with white wimples and brown veils over their heads, never raised their voices, were gentle and loving, and always had a smile for every child. All the children wore pleated chocolate brown gaberdine tunics over white blouses. I liked school and worked hard at my lessons. I remember bringing home good record cards. But what I remember most was our playtime.

The nuns told us with a smile that running around and getting hot was "unladylike, and a lady never sweats." "Remember," they said, "poise and dignity show good posture and behaviour." But they believed in exercising a child's imagination.

At the midmorning break, two nuns pulled out a large ornate wooden box, which looked like a pirate's chest. Inside was the treasure: scarves and hats, boots and flashy buckles, old ornately inscribed books, maps of the world, glittering strings of beads, gold, silver, and pearls. There were even swash-buckling swords and daggers. We created theatre every day.

After playtime, it was lunch, a time for our stimulated minds to rest and become calm before returning to our studies. Everyone, including the nuns, sat quietly on benches outside the classroom and ate lunch. Mummy always made me a special dark chocolate sandwich; she grated the chocolate over the creamy butter spread thickly on homemade bread.

On my first day, the nuns assigned me to an older girl called Angela. We sat together and I followed her around and learnt what to do. She became my best friend in school until the day she stepped on her father's upturned rake and punctured the bottom of her foot. She was out of school for over six weeks. I missed her terribly, especially when I was stung by a bee on the palm of my hand.

The children made fun of me, saying that my hand looked like a bullfrog's throat. Without Angela, I had to pretend it was fun to chase the other children with my swollen hand. During this time, I made friends with Monica and her blonde-haired boys, Graham and Thomas.

Looking back, I realize I became a tomboy that year. Outside of school, Graham, Thomas, and I became a team. We were always up to some scheme or other. We climbed trees, begging the friendly White plantation farmers and Black labourers to give us rope and wood to make swings and ladders.

When the workers were collecting honey from nearby hives, we would come and beg for some honeycomb. It was warm and dripping with delicious sweetness. We chewed until the comb became a pink mass of chewing gum consistency. We also enjoyed the cashew harvesting; it is a strange fruit. The nut, encased in a hard shell, grows outside of the soft fleshy fruit, the cashew apple. The fruit was not suitable for shipping; when ripe, its yellowy-orange or red paper-thin skins burst when picked. The nuts were the only part harvested. The labourers laughed at us for wanting to eat the sicky, sweet fruit but still let us help ourselves to a few pieces as they were laid out on large sheets to dry. Occasionally, we had a chance to have freshly roasted cashew nuts. They were delicious; the raw nuts are poisonous.

I sometimes went with Daddy to the lime mill in Foxes Bay as a special treat. It was a water processing plant for the West Indian sour limes. I loved it there.

The native women collected the ripe fruit from the farms in baskets and brought them to the mill in wagons. These wagons backed up to a wide platform where the fruit rolled down to a rotary washer, which sprayed pressurized water over the fruit to remove any dirt and grime. A slow-moving conveyor belt pushed the fruit along for final inspection and the removal of damaged fruit before transportation to the crusher.

It was the next stage I loved best. Now ready for processing, the fruit tumbled into a wooden chute and down between large rollers covered with perforated zinc. The tangy air became pungent, almost choking me at the back of my throat and burning my eyes, but the smell was delicious. A big wheel, turned by shirtless Black men chanting in a mesmerizing tone, kept the rollers moving at a steady speed.

When I asked Mummy what language they were singing in, she said it was probably a mixture of French and English Creole. The pressed juice ran into vats made from white oak to prevent tainting the juice and oil.

After a settling period, the liquid was clarified by heating, to separate the juice from the oil, and then siphoned into separate large barrels and made ready for shipping. Sometimes I was lucky enough to be there when a man hammered in the final corks. I felt exhilarated by the strength and force of the man swinging his mallet high into the air and bringing it down with a singular thunk, sealing the cork tight in the barrel. Workers rolled the barrels down a ramp into small boats, taking them out to the ships waiting to leave for England.

Our first Christmas in Montserrat was quiet; we had only been on the island for a few months. Daddy was busy settling into a new job, and we didn't know many people. Mrs. Shand, our neighbour, invited us to her house for dinner. It was the strangest meal I ever had. She had cooked a hen and arranged the unlaid eggs on a plate around the chicken in order of the varying stages of development, from a whole egg, with its shell still on, to a yolk, no bigger than my little finger. I was fascinated and dinner became a biology lesson!

Afterward, Mrs. Shand lit the candles on her pretty Christmas tree. It was covered with tiny red glass balls and silver tinsel hanging from the branches. We exchanged a few handmade gifts. Mummy gave Mrs. Shand a handmade knitted tea cosy, and I had a knitted rabbit with a removable pinafore dress. We ate Mummy's Christmas pudding with custard for dessert and sang hymns and Christmas carols while Mrs. Shand played her piano.

After such a happy day, I was unprepared for the trauma that was about to happen.

An Unholy Terrors

"Mummy, there's a crowd of people dancing in the street. Can I go outside, please?" I asked excitedly. "Please? I'll be really careful; I won't go into the street, I promise."

"It's a carnival," Mummy said without much enthusiasm in her voice.

"What's a carnival?" I asked eagerly.

"High jinks and craziness, that's what it is," Mummy said, pressing her lips tightly together.

The loud steel band calypso music filled the air. It was a floating mass of bright colours, blues, reds, and golds, swirling and moving as far as I could see. It was beautiful! There were big Black men, their skins glistening in the sun, playing the steel drums, as they stood on platforms moving slowly up the street in front of the dancers. It was a powerful and mesmerizing sound.

"Damn darkie music," Daddy said, going into his room and closing the door.

I shivered. Daddy's temper was powerful and always made me afraid. Still, I pleaded, "Please, please can I go outside, Mummy?"

"Take care, just stay up on the embankment. Be a good girl, and do not go down into the road. There are too many excited people out there in the street. God only knows what they might do."

I ran outside, happy and eager to watch the exotic parade of people passing under the gnarled old tamarind tree. I had never heard calypso music before. I felt its hypnotic effects as I leaned my tummy against the old tree trunk, motionlessly watching the parade; it was exciting, magical at that moment.

Walking behind every steel band were Black women, boys, and girls, dressed in elaborate and exotic dresses and pants in brilliant colours of reds, oranges, yellows, and blues. The women balanced huge headdresses of ornate, sequined feathers, flowers, and fruit on their heads. They

21

were singing, dancing, and twirling, lifting their skirts high in the air. I was startled to see so much naked skin. I didn't think Mummy would like that.

I probably had my mouth open. "Catching flies," Mummy would say. My eyes, the only part of me moving, darted left and right as I tried to take in everything at once. I was totally absorbed in the sights and sounds around me. I was fascinated by everything until my eyes caught a movement to my right, one that would change my view of this incredible parade forever.

"Aayeee!" an ear-splitting sound pierced the air.

I froze, staring into the red and black eyes of a terrifying demon running towards me. My brain seared every detail in that split second. He had long, black, knotted-hair and hessian (burlap) sacking over his body, tied around his middle with rope and chains. Even before his second scream, my mind exploded with fear. I ran with explosive speed up to the house and threw myself full tilt into Mummy's arms as she came out of the front door.

"Mummy, Mummy, the devil is out there. He's going to get me," I screamed.

"Hush, hush, dear," she said. "Just come inside and let me shut the door."

From the living room, my face buried in a pillow, I heard the door open again and Mummy saying in an unusually loud and brusk voice, "Get out of my garden, you are trespassing."

I did not go outside again that day or look out of the window. "Please close the shutters, Mummy," I begged. "I don't want him to get me." I was terrified, convinced I had narrowly escaped being swallowed up by the devil.

"It's all right, Jane," Mummy reassured me "He's gone now. You are safe here."

"Damn foolishness," I heard Daddy mutter as he came out of the bedroom and went into the bathroom. "Never trust a darkie."

With the certainty of a young child, I knew the devil was out to get me. I knew I hadn't really disobeyed Mummy, but I did know she disapproved of the music and dancing, and I had gone outside anyway. I should have heeded what Daddy often said, "Your mother knows best."

I remember Mummy laughing at me and telling me not to worry.

"The devil only comes for the wicked," she said.

Still, I was not reassured. I developed a fever the next day, probably brought on by my fear of the devil. I stayed in bed. Daddy went to work, as usual, coming home for lunch to see how I was doing. Mummy brought me my meals on a tray for a few days but then told me that I must get up and come to the table to eat.

"You'll be starting school again soon and need to be ready."

Mummy never talked about the demon again, but it was the beginning of a long relationship with the fear of death and the devil.

I would be thirteen years of age before a friend persuaded me to watch another carnival.

—:• ⊕ •:—

Isolated from other West Indian cultures, Monserrat owed its major cultural influence to predominantly African and local Creole sources. The island's traditional stories were derived from folk magic, love, and historical occurrences. In the 1950s the "Street Jam" or Carnival, was a lively street celebration that took place from December 26th to January 1st. calypso singers took this opportunity to vent their feelings about the local government in power at the time, British dominance, or to raise awareness about other happenings on the island.

The devil, or "Jab Jab," in the Creole language, represents evil and temptation. He is a well-documented character in Carnival celebrations who smears his body with grease, tar, or mud; he paints his face white and wears horns and chains. The red eyes I saw were probably the effect of the black skin and white paint accentuating the eyes.

When the British supplanted the French in the islands, they continued Carnival as a privileged ruling class celebration. Masked balls and dances were held on the four days before Lent. With the abolition of slavery, the freed people took Carnival to the streets incorporating their African origins. By 1872, the colonial authorities, afraid of the power and force of the people's culture, decided to ban the celebrations. This caused the Carnival Riots in February 1879.

There wasn't a Carnival in Barbados, where I lived first, like on the other islands. The conservative nature of the White people in the 1950s and 1960s caused an inhibition to play Jump Up in the streets. These celebrations were reinvented in 1978, long after I had left the islands.

Hurricane Audrey

Hurricane Audrey hit Monserrat on 26th June 1957. It went on to cause much damage and loss of lives in Louisiana, and in the Gulf of Mexico. I was seven then and remembered hearing the warnings on the radio. Daddy battened down the wooden shutters on the windows while I helped Mummy prepare for living out the storm indoors.

We removed objects from the walls and put drawers on the floor. We spread blankets under and over the top of the large dining room table for protection and to muffle the sound of the storm in case we needed to sleep. Mummy sat rocking in her chair, her fingers crossed, counting from each flash of lighting until the thunder crashed. It measured the distance between us and the storm. Twice, the lightning and thunder flashed and echoed simultaneously, which meant the storm was right overhead and the noise from the thunder was deafening. I lay under the table with my teddy bear, reading my storybook and feeling safe. But I also listened to Mummy counting the seconds between the crash and flash of thunder and lightning; Daddy was in his room reading the newspaper.

The electricity in the storm passed quickly, and I heard Mummy sigh with relief from her rocking chair and said, "God be praised."

I fell asleep under the table listening to the rain falling on the galvanized roof. It sounded like the drums in a steel band; the rhythm was soothing.

When the storm abated, there were bees everywhere. Lightning had hit the gnarled tree, breaking it off at the waist and spilling hundreds of bees from their hive. Daddy wouldn't let me go outside, but I watched from the front window as the bees buzzed crazily around the broken hive. I felt sorry for those tiny creatures and their lost home. Daddy was more worried about the cable pole hanging inches from our roof.

"Fetch me my Wellingtons, Janie," Daddy said in a concerned voice. "I need to fix that pole now. If it falls, it will rip our roof off." He pulled on his rubber boots and went outside, still in his pyjamas.

Life went back to normal when Daddy removed the shutters, except for Mummy's sad face. A lot of silver packed away in small boxes; ornate teaspoons is what memory brings to mind, had gone missing.

"Never trust a darkie," Daddy said.

He assumed our servants had stolen the silver, but we never found out what had happened.

We were not wealthy, but we did have a couple of servants come weekly to help Mummy. It was considered the right way to boost the island's economy by hiring the local Black people to carry out certain tasks. They did laundry, house cleaning, and cleaning the silver, which most colonial families had in those times.

The Doctor Next Door

Mummy received an elegant invitation in the mail, requesting Mrs. Moller and her daughter's company for afternoon tea. It was from our neighbour, Dr. Huntley. I thought it rather strange to receive such a formal invitation when she could've just knocked on our door! But I was excited because Mummy told me to put on my pretty Sunday dress and be on my best behaviour.

I loved the doctor's parlour and furniture, which Mummy called "chintzy," and the thick patterned carpets, but I didn't like her two black cats. They sat on the arms of Dr. Huntley's chair and stared unblinkingly at me. I felt afraid; they looked evil. Dr. Huntley's china was similar to ours, on which she served tiny fancy iced cakes. "Fairy parcels," I exclaimed.

"Really, child!" Dr. Huntley admonished me. "They are called *petit-four glacé*. I had them sent from France. Would you like one?" she said, holding out the plate of cakes.

"Yes, please," I said, taking one carefully between my thumb and forefinger and placing it on my napkin. I wanted to show Dr. Huntley that I knew how to behave properly. I wanted a second cake to take home and show Daddy, but I didn't ask because I could tell Mummy wanted to leave; she had a tight-lipped smile and her eyes glinted. Later, I overheard her telling Daddy about our "uppity neighbour."

A week or so later, while outside playing on the swing I'd made from string and cardboard, Dr. Huntley's face appeared over the top of her fence.

"Would you like to have tea with me again, little girl? You can have another one of those — what did you call them, fairy parcels?"

"Yes, please," I said, surprised but delighted that she wanted me to have tea with her. Maybe this time, I could ask if I could take one home for Daddy. I followed her happily into the house.

"Why don't we take your cake into the parlour," Dr. Huntley said, placing a pale yellow iced petit four onto a plate; the cake was decorated with pink ribbons and blue forget-me-nots.

"So, tell me, little girl — "

"My name is Jane." I interrupted quietly.

"All right, Jane, why don't you sit in that chair, and I'll sit over here. Now, tell me about yourself and your mother."

I didn't know what to say, plus I was having difficulty balancing a plate on my lap and eating the little cake. Dr. Huntley's cats sat on the arms of my chair, and whenever I lifted my hand to my mouth, they hissed at me. I thought Dr. Huntley was going to push the cats off the chair when she leaned forward; instead, she said, "Tell me, Jane, how old is your mother?"

"She's ninety-nine," I replied.

What she said next made me freeze with panic. I dropped the unfinished cake, leapt out of the chair, and ran out the door.

"Mummy, Mummy," I sobbed as I stumbled home. I was so upset that I didn't notice the scratches on my arms made by the cats as I had jumped out of the chair, nor the nail I ripped off my big toe as I'd stumbled over the concrete step in my haste to get inside our house.

Mummy bathed my arms and put iodine on my ripped toenail before she asked me why I was so upset. "Now, let's have some tea and biscuits and you can tell me what all that fuss was about."

"It was awful, Mummy," I cried. "She asked me how old you were and when I told her, she laughed and said you couldn't be my mother. But you are, aren't you?"

"Slowly dear, slowly, who is 'she,' and what did you say to her?"

"Dr. Huntley invited me for one of those fairy parcels, but she wanted to know how old you were, and I answered as you told me."

"Oh," Mummy said in a strange voice. "That hoity-toity lady, she needs to mind her own business. I feel like going over there and giving her a piece of my mind," she said, making as if to get up.

"Please don't leave me, Mummy. You are my mother, aren't you?" I asked again.

"We'll have a little talk about that before you go to bed when you are not so upset. But I don't see any other Mummy taking care of you, do you?"

"I am glad." I sighed as I cuddled into Mummy's soft arms.

Later, Mummy explained that after all her other children had grown up and left home, she'd felt lonely. She had decided to visit her daughters in England and while there, adopted a baby girl. "When a mother has a baby, Jane, she doesn't know whether it will be a girl or a boy until it is born." Mummy began explaining.

"But how does the Mummy get the baby?" I asked.

"That is a question for another time, dear. Be quiet now, and I will explain about you becoming my little girl."

⁙

Mummy was always reticent to explain the details of a complicated situation. She didn't tell me much more, except that I had been born to a person who could not keep me.

Mummy also told me that my two names meant: Jane, chosen by God, and Elizabeth, child of God. As a protected and loved seven-year-old, I believed every word she told me and it was enough. I trusted Mummy and Daddy to always be there for me.

Mummy did not explain her reasoning for saying her age was "ninety-nine."

Later, when I understood things better, I realised that parents often lie about their age, but generally they reduce their age. I thought it was probably Mummy's contrary sense of humour which caused her to increase her age. It was her way to make a statement against the ridiculousness of vanity.

Wong — A Special Kitten

When I came home from school, I was surprised that Mummy wasn't standing in her usual place at the front door. Was something wrong, I thought, as I ran into the house. Mummy held up a warning finger even before I spoke. Curled in her lap, I saw a tiny chocolate-coloured ball of fur. I hadn't had a cat since we lived in Barbados. I still missed Moony terribly. He had been a large ginger tomcat who would jump onto my shoulders when I stood in the garden and called him.

"Go change out of your school uniform, dear, and I'll tell you all about it while we have a cup of tea and a slice of the chocolate cake I made today."

"Yummy, yummy," I said as I rushed into the bedroom. I loved Mummy's chocolate cake; it was special. Mummy mixed and baked it all in the same tin. Flour and lots of chocolate powder went in the tin first. Mummy made a well in each corner. She poured oil in one, into another, she put lovely golden brown sugar; sticky and sweet, and into the third well, she broke an egg, fresh from our chickens. Into the last, she put vinegar! The first time I watched Mummy make the cake, I was terribly worried that the vinegar would spoil the taste, but it didn't.

I undid my brown lace-up shoes; I only wore them for school. I undid my heavy brown gaberdine tunic and stepping out of it, left it on the floor. The buttons on the white blouse with its pretty puffed sleeves always took a long time, and my hands fumbled even more in my haste. I slipped a clean cotton dress over my cotton vest and panties and went into the bathroom to wash my hands. No point in missing that part — I might not get any cake!

When I returned to the sitting room, Mummy had already poured the tea and a warm slice of chocolate cake sat on a plate waiting for me.

In between bits of cake, I asked, "How did you get this funny-looking kitty? Can I hold him, please? Oh! Is his tail broken?" Mummy began

30

her story as she always did, from the beginning, smiling as she did so.

"I answered a knock at the front door. It was a Chinaman, standing in the rain, with this poor little mite's legs hanging down dismally over his hand. The kitten opened its tiny mouth, and no sound came out. 'Lord, love us,' I said to the Chinaman. 'Give me the little mite, and I'll give it some warm milk.' He grinned saying, 'You takee, make happy, yes?' What was I to say? So now we have a kitten in the home again."

I was so happy I jumped up, hugging Mummy and kitten together. "Thank you, thank you."

"Alrighty, alrighty, git away with yer fussing and go find a box and blanket to make a bed for him," Mummy said. Waving her hand in the direction of my bedroom, she said, "He can sleep under your bed at night if you're a good girl."

We called him Wong. He grew into a beautiful Seal-point Siamese cat with a strange tail that went down from his body for a couple of inches and curled back on itself. At the very tip of the tail was a knot.

"He is a throwback," Mummy said when I asked her about his funny tail.

"The original Siamese cats were guardians of the Egyptian Royal Palace. When the royal family was forced to flee, the cats curled their tails around the crown jewels and knotted the tip through the royal seal."

I loved the story. I later learnt Siamese cats were considered rare and reserved only for royalty back in the days of the Egyptian kings and queens. The cats were thought to possess rare powers of intercession for the departed souls and were fed only the best foods and slept on the softest silk cushions.

Wong lived and moved with us as a family for the rest of his life, long after I was a teenager and had left the islands.

A Very Special Christmas

Our last Christmas in Montserrat was different from all other Christmases. It was so special that it has become immortalized in my memory. Daddy must have made some money that year because we had guests come to the house: my best friends, Graham and Thomas, and their mother, Monica. When Monica left home, she travelled in a bath chair, which looked like a rolling caned chaise. I thought she looked like a china doll. Our neighbour, Mrs. Shand, was there and a few government officials whom Daddy worked with. He served small glasses of sherry to all the grown-ups except Mummy, who never drank any alcohol. I was glad when my best friend from school, Angela, dropped by with her parents for a quick visit. Mummy served individual homemade mincemeat pies with cream.

On Christmas morning, I woke up before it was light. I felt around for the pillowcase I used instead of a stocking I'd put at the bottom of my bed the night before. It was exciting to grope for the pillowcase in the dark; I tried to imagine what surprises it held this year. Reaching deep inside, I pulled out an odd-shaped package. In the dark, it felt soft in places and hard in others. I crept out of bed and went to Mummy's room. She always allowed me to open one present, whenever I woke up on Christmas Day. "Mummy, Mummy," I whispered, "Can I open this present, please?"

She opened her eyes immediately and sat up. It felt like she was waiting for me to come into the room. "Okie dokie dear, open it up. Let's see what it is."

The present was a furry monkey sitting on his haunches with a red cap on his head and brass cymbals in his hands. "It's adorable," I squealed. There was a large fan-shaped key sticking out in the back of his fur. I went to turn the key.

"Nope," Mummy said quietly, "Winding that key will have to wait

32

until breakfast. Now you go ahead and climb back into bed," she said, kissing me on the forehead, "and I'll see you in the morning."

"Nighty night, Mummy. Happy Christmas." I said and crept back to my room and went to sleep.

In the morning, I searched through the pillowcase for other gifts. There were a few chocolate gold coins and oranges, some of which I ate. Along with the chocolates, I found a set of six handkerchiefs with beautifully embroidered blue forget-me-nots around a satin-stitched 'J' in one corner, a silky yellow petticoat, and white socks for school. Although Mummy made everything except the socks, I still believed everything came directly from Father Christmas. After finishing one of my oranges, I wound up the monkey and took it into the dining room.

"Happy Christmas, Mummy, Daddy. Look what I got. Isn't he cute?"

"That sure is something," Daddy said.

Mummy laughed and said, "Wong isn't too happy with your noisy little monkey though. Look at him."

Wong, his back arched, had leapt onto a chair by the Christmas tree. He didn't make a sound, but his pupils were huge. I laughed, put down the toy, and petted Wong. I then continued to wind and rewind my new toy. Eventually, Wong curled up in the tree skirt and went to sleep. I sat the monkey on the table while we ate our breakfast. It was a full English breakfast for high days and holidays: liver and bacon, eggs, fried rice, fried tomatoes, toast and marmalade.

After breakfast, we opened our presents that were under the tree; it was so pretty and sparkling with glass ornaments. Daddy received knitted socks. Mummy had a book, and I had a new Bunnikin bowl.

"You'd better put that monkey toy away for now," Daddy said. "We'll have guests arriving shortly, and you wouldn't want anyone to step on it, would you?"

"Oh no, Daddy! I'll put him away." I had never forgotten his anger when I was much younger and he'd had tripped over something I had left on the floor.

I remember little of the main course we ate at Christmas, but I loved Christmas pudding and cake. Mummy made the Christmas pudding and cake in September with dried fruit and nut mixtures, most of which came from our family in England and America, plus molasses and eggs. The only difference between the cake and pudding was the fat used and how

Mummy cooked it. The cake used butter and was baked. After the cake cooled, Mummy covered it with marzipan and thick, crunchy royal icing made from beaten egg whites and sugar. She then rolled and smoothed the mix over the cake. Mummy stored the cake in a tin until Christmas, when a pretty-patterned ribbon, which we used every year, was added around the sides of the cake.

Mummy used beef suet instead of butter in the pudding. While mixing, she added the sterling silver trinkets she had received as a wedding gift years ago. It was then wrapped in a thick cloth and steamed for hours until it was very dark in colour.

During the week Mummy made the pudding, she invited visitors who came by the house to stir the mixture and make a wish for Christmas. I invited Graham and Thomas to come and stir in their wishes. They thought it was fun.

I believed it made us all very special when we ate the cake and shared it with friends. Christmas Day, Mummy steamed the pudding for a few more hours, and we ate it hot with cream after our dinner.

Boxing Day, the day after Christmas, started in the usual quiet way. We didn't have a special breakfast, but we ate together. It was a government holiday and Daddy didn't work. We had cold meats and pickles for lunch and dinner, followed by mincemeat pies for dessert. We had Christmas cake with tea in the afternoon. Daddy read the paper and twiddled with the radio. Mummy shut her ears and read, pretending she wasn't annoyed by the whining sound. She worked on her patchwork quilt in the afternoon; it was a hexagonal Grannie's Flower Garden quilt. It was destined for the Canadian Expo the following year.

The house was relatively quiet and peaceful, except for me singing or playing with my toys or Wong. I was teaching him new tricks with one of the glass balls off the tree; it was one I knew wasn't precious to Mummy. When the ball rolled behind the tree, I saw it — a large wrapped box with my name on it.

"Mummy, Mummy, there is a large present for me under the tree. Can I open it?"

"Why, of course, dear, if it has your name on it. Who is it from?"

I quickly pulled the box out from under the tree, turning it over and around but saw no name other than my own written in large script. "I don't know; it only has my name printed on it." What if? I thought, my whole body shivering with excitement, "Do you think Father Christmas left it? He must have come twice if he did!"

"You would be very special if he did," Mummy said, her eyes sparkling, her whole face smiling.

"By Jove, you are one very lucky little girl, Janie." Daddy said with a chuckle.

I was very excited about discovering the gift; it was a boxed set of Beatrix Potter stories. Every morning for the next week, I jumped out of bed and rushed to the living room to check under the tree, just in case another present should appear.

The Boxing-Day* special never happened again but the magic of that day has stayed with me for the rest of my life. When the calypso music echoed in the street once again, I stayed resolutely inside, making a tent of my bedcovers and reading my special gifts.

Footnote:
* Boxing-Day was a Commonwealth holiday and was originally marked by the giving of special Christmas boxes to service workers.

Last Days in Monserrat

Coming into my bedroom shortly after the day of our second Carnival in Monserrat, Mummy peeled back the sheets on my bed, saying firmly, "Get up out of there. It isn't time to go to bed. Hiding from your fears never solved any problem."

"I'm scared, Mummy. I don't want the devil to get me. I'm afraid he'll steal my soul."

"What on earth are you talking about, Jane? God doesn't let the devil take a child's soul. Who told you such nonsense?"

"The nuns are always saying to be on guard against the devil, and we must go to church to confess our sins," I said with tears running down my face.

"Stuff and nonsense," Mummy snorted.

I thought I could see the steam coming out of her ears and nose!

"The devil isn't something you can see, dear. A child doesn't have sins to confess. Children are innocent and pure. God loves children, remember the beatitudes? 'Blessed are the pure in heart, for they shall see God.'"

"We don't go to church, though, Mummy. How can God love us?"

"Of course he does dear. The Bible says, 'Where two or three are gathered together in my name, there am I in their midst.' It doesn't say we have to meet in a church. Jane, do you remember that your names mean something special too?" Mummy said with a smile in her eyes.

"Tell me again, what do they mean, Mummy?" I asked, looking up and wiping the tears from my eyes.

"Jane means, 'Child of God,' and Elizabeth means 'Chosen by God,' so you see you are protected all the time."

"Oh!" was all I said at the time, but I suddenly felt different. Hearing the meaning of my names again made me feel stronger.

"Enough of this foolishness. The devil does find work for idle hands,

36

so get up out of this bed and go do something with your young life."

"I'll try to be brave. What shall I do? I don't want to go outside where I can hear all that noise."

"Why don't you scoot out back, and go across the scrubland to play with your friends, Graham and Thomas?"

"OK, Mummy, I'll keep to the trees. I'll feel safer. I'll be back in time for tea," I said, throwing my arms around her soft neck and giving her a quick squeeze before she had a chance to stop me.

"That's enough of that. Don't get soppy now," Mummy replied, shaking my arms loose as she stood up. "Off you go now and have fun."

I put on my shoes and ran out the back door. I spent most of the day playing hide and seek with my friends in their old stone barn.

Sadly, something bad did happen that day. As I stepped off the ladder onto the rafters of the old barn, I heard Thomas shout. "We're not allowed up there." A second or two later, the boards gave way underneath my feet. I fell about ten feet to the floor below with a sickening thud, knocking all the breath out of me.

At first, I couldn't stand up, but when the boys wanted to get help, I said, "No, just help me up, I can do it." We stayed a while longer playing I-Spy while sitting in the large stone windows, looking out across the fields.

I don't remember how I got home. The next day, my left leg swelled to twice its normal size and I couldn't walk. I don't remember going to a hospital, and I know I didn't break any bones. What I do remember was my leg bandaged from thigh to ankle.

Daddy carried me from the bedroom to the dining room in the mornings for breakfast and then to the living room before leaving for work. I spent most of my days on the sofa doing the things I loved: reading, doing puzzles, or colouring picture books. Occasionally, Wong would curl up on my lap. Usually, he slept right next to Mummy's rocking chair, his tongue sticking out just a little bit.

If I was bored, or Mummy thought I should do something more productive, she'd hand me the scissors. "Here, why don't you cut the hexagonal papers and then tack the patches of material over each paper as I've shown you how to do."

Mummy would later hem the patches together for her Grannie's Flower Garden quilt. Before we all left Monserrat, Mummy boxed the finished quilt and sent it to Canada for the Expo. I have little memory of doing any school work.

During my recovery, Daddy carried me back to my bed after dinner. My fear of the devil remained, manifesting in nightmares and a terrifying fear of death. But now, I had a weapon with which to fight my fear. I'd think about the meaning of my names to calm myself and go back to sleep. In the future, I would lean heavily on this knowledge whenever I was unhappy or afraid.

I resolved to tell Mummy that I wanted to go to church when I recovered. I knew just saying my prayers at night didn't feel enough. I never got to ask because we left Montserrat for St. Vincent, about a month later, immediately after I could walk again, and life was difficult for a while.

• • •

We sailed out of the Plymouth Harbor, Monserrat, in late January 1958.

Daddy had secured a cabin for the three of us and our personal belongings on the *Maracas Bay*. I was sad to go; I had enjoyed having friends to play with. I knew Mummy would miss Mrs. Shand. But Daddy's job was finished and he was eager to move on and find something new. What he wanted was his own farm.

As animals were not allowed on boats, Mummy carried Wong in a double-lidded basket, the handle over her arm. Colonialism was still a strong power on the island. It wasn't usual for a local Black authority figure to question an older White woman in those days. Mummy could be formidable when she chose to be. Asked if she would open the basket for the customs officer, she refused, saying it was only our food for the journey. Wong never meowed or tried to climb out of the basket. He lay quietly under a heavily folded tablecloth, just in case a customs officer should be audacious enough to open the basket lid.

The *Maracas Bay* was a cargo ship; we had the captain's cabin, which was tiny and only had one bunk. Daddy wedged the suitcases and trunks across the cabin floor to prevent damage to our bodies and luggage. In the space left, we laid down on the floor, fully clothed; Mummy and I in dresses and Daddy in his khaki shorts. Our heads were against the bunk, and our feet faced the door; we were braced crosswise against the roll of the boat. The double-lidded basket lay between Mummy and me.

All night we rolled and pitched; I was afraid we might drown. All I could think of was the shipwreck of the *Nellie Bywater*; my sister, Anne, survived, but not her fiancé. I worried what would happen if we capsized? Wong would be lost, I couldn't swim, and Mummy was afraid of the water; that only left Daddy, and how could he save us all?

To hide my fears and help me sleep, I imagined I was on a high seas adventure. Daddy's snoring was reassuring, occasionally interrupted with a muttered, "God damn and blast," when he banged into a box or something. It was comforting to hear Mummy's praying under her breath. I knew she kept her fingers crossed all the time. Mummy once told me that she liked to cover all her bases; she applied prayer and superstition. I felt secure but not safe. I believed Mummy's prayers would take us all to heaven if we drowned.

It was the first and only time we sailed on a flat bottom boat. I remember the urgency of the radio calls and how frightened I was by the pitch and roll of the vessel as if it was yesterday. "*Maracas-Bay, Maracas-Bay*, calling the *Pensi-Cola Bay*, calling the *Pensi-Cola Bay*."

For many years afterwards, I would invent games of being at sea, calling the *Pensi-Cola Bay*.

Jane with Wong at Sunningdale

Jane, Lorna, Wong, and Bingo at Sunningdale

ST VINCENT

1958–1964

On Firm Ground

After two days of rolling around in a flat bottom boat, standing on firm ground was delightful. We disembarked after tidying up and putting on clean clothes.

Always a must, Mummy said, "Never lower one's standards, always keep your head up, and look another person in the eye."

I was anxious going through customs. We only had a few personal belongings, but I was scared that the customs officer might open the basket and see we had a cat. I never doubted Mummy's ability to keep Wong hidden; she carried the two-lidded basket over her arm, but I was afraid. I kept my eyes on the ground most of the time. When the Black man in his crisp white uniform asked Mummy what she had in the basket, I held my breath, squeezing my eyes shut.

"None of your business; these are my personal belongings," she said politely, looking the uniformed man in the eye. I looked up and smiled.

I was exhilarated as he waved us through, with a "Good day to you, Marm."

We caught a taxi to Arnos Vale, where we would spend a week or so with Aunty Gussie while Daddy looked for a house for us. Aunty Gussie was Daddy's sister, whom I had never met. The first to meet us was a very old Black man, whom Mummy greeted with a smile while Daddy paid the taxi driver.

"Good to see you again, Conrad. Life's been treating you well, I hope?"

"Yes, Missus Moller, very well thank ye, Marm."

Then looking toward Daddy, he said, "I'll take care of the bags, Mr. Moller. Gertrude will come and show you into the sitting room; the Missus be waiting there."

He turned back to Mummy with a wide grin and leaned behind her, "This must be the young un'? Mistress Jane?"

43

"Yes, Conrad. Come out from behind me, Jane, say hello to Conrad. I've known him since he was a young man."

I moved a couple of steps from behind Mummy's skirt; however, I stayed close. "Hello."

Conrad had a very black face with deep wrinkles, his backbone curved forward slightly, and his wiry hair was full of crinkly white flecks. He seems friendly enough, I thought.

Daddy was moving towards the front steps, "Come on, Edie," he said impatiently to Mummy. "We better not keep Gussie waiting."

"We'll talk again later, Conrad; I'd like to know how your daughter's doing. Come on, Jane, let's go and introduce you to your aunt."

Gertrude met us at the front door. She was a very old Black woman; she had a few strands of white hair sticking out from beneath her faded head-kerchief and had as many wrinkles as Conrad. Mummy was pleased to see her and greeted her warmly.

"The Missus asked me to show you to your rooms so you can freshen up first. She'll meet you in the sitting room when you are ready."

"Typical," Daddy said under his breath.

As Gertrude showed us up the dark wood curving staircase to our rooms, I whispered, "This house is so big, Mummy; I'll get lost going downstairs on my own."

"Better not get used to it," Daddy said. "We'll only be staying here for a little while, just enough time to find a house and no more. Better instruct the child how not to offend my sister, Edie."

"Clem, please be gracious. Children have large ears."

This kind of talk gave me collywobbles in my stomach. It made me unsure of myself. "Might Auntie Gussie not like me, Mummy?"

"Don't be silly, dear. Of course, she will. Daddy's just tired, and he knows that your aunt likes things done properly. Remember, sit with your dress over your knees, only speak when you are spoken to, and you'll get on fine with her."

When Gertrude left us for a moment to fetch water for washing, I looked around. We had two rooms, each with two beds. Each bed had a mosquito net hanging from a round hoop hooked to the ceiling. A dark red carpet, "Indian," Mummy said, covered the centre of the dark wood floor, polished to a deep shine. The furniture was dark mahogany, with ornate golden trimmings. Two white linen towels hung from the rails of a chest of drawers. On the dressing table sat a large, flowered bowl.

Gertrude returned with a large jug of warm water; it matched the bowl. We washed our faces and hands; Mummy dabbed a few drops of Eau de Cologne behind her ears, and we went downstairs.

Auntie Gussie was tall, beautiful, and elegant. Her white hair combed into waves, framed her face, 1920s style. Her dress looked rich and felt soft and silky when she hugged me. I was surprised by her affection and stepped back quickly when she let go of me.

The sitting room had large windows looking out into the garden on one side and down over the valley on the other side. The furniture was stiff, upright, chintz-covered chairs and a chaise lounge; it looked like something I'd seen in an expensive magazine. Tea was served in beautiful flower patterned fine china. It tasted strange, not like the tea we had at home. While Auntie Gussie poured the tea, I quietly checked out the rest of the room; she even had a piano. Maybe I could learn to play.

The next day, I began exploring the house and grounds. On the north side of the house, which didn't get much sunshine, was a large irregular area; a semi-circle of rough grass littered with old tree stumps. On the furthest edge of the grass, a stone wall came up from the steep driveway; it was a long drop. Running alongside the house was a three-foot-wide concrete ditch with a four-foot drop. I could see, but not touch, the long narrow windows of the cellar. When I went down into the cellar from the other side of the house, I couldn't find those windows.

I asked Gertrude about the windows. She only said, "It's locked up. A dark and dangerous place. No one's allowed there anymore." I was curious but accepted what she told me and didn't attempt to go into that part of the cellar for the next few years. Not until after we moved to our house in Calliaqua.

Auntie Gussie loved dogs and always had a few around the place. There are three dogs that I remember. One was a gorgeous spaniel called Reddy. She also had a prize American bulldog with an enormous head and short legs. Auntie Gussie spent a lot of money on purchasing the bulldog to breed. Unfortunately, he turned out to be a sheep killer, and he was shot. The last dog was a boxer named Tessa. Auntie Gussie also had a beautiful macaw parrot called Dan, whom Conrad took care of. Dan was the terror of all who worked on the estate.

I didn't get to know Conrad or Gertrude well during our short stay at

Arnos Vale House, but a couple of times I sneaked downstairs and visited Conrad in his tiny shack under the stairs. I was fascinated. I would get to know and enjoy Conrad's company a few years later when we moved back to Arnos Vale and lived at the second bungalow.

I was beginning to enjoy roaming Arnos Vale house, with all its bedrooms and secret places to hide, when Daddy came home and told us it was time to move.

Little House on the Hill

Our new home, which we called the house on the hill, was small and simple. It felt like it could have fitted into Auntie Gussie's sitting room with room to spare. The house sat at the bottom of a long mud and gravel driveway, which ran downhill from the tarred road to stop just before the front steps. There was a tiny flower garden on either side of the steps, then a verandah running the width of the house.

The front door opened onto the living room: the bedrooms were on the left, with a tiny bathroom between the two rooms. The kitchen was a partitioned strip at the back of the living room. The outside wall had a large window facing south, looking down through the valley into Kingstown. It made the room very bright. It also had a large walk-in larder on the left, as we came in from the living room, for storing dry food. Next to the larder was the back door, and under the window there was a smooth, painted wood counter with a deep white enamel sink set into it. A wood cook-stove was in the far corner. A lot more stone stairs ran down from the back door because the house was on a slope. At the bottom, a small flat area was carved out of the grass for planting. The rest of the property was rough grass, running down the valley.

Without a refrigerator, butter, cheese, milk, and sometimes meat was kept in a dug-out cold cellar under the east side of the house. I loved to fetch food from there for Mummy. I'd have to put my whole arm into the smooth-sided dirt cave to get the still hard, fresh packs of butter.

We hadn't been in the house very long before there was a terrible storm one night. The next morning, Mummy called out to Daddy and me to come quickly and be careful as we came into the living room because there was water all over the floor.

The house was built in the path of the floodwaters coming off the hill. There was a torrent of rainwater coming down the driveway, over the low front steps, under the front door, running through the living room, and out through the back door. It was scary seeing all that water rushing through the house, but by the time we'd grabbed brooms and mops, swept and pushed the water through the house, we were all laughing hard.

"Well, now we have a clean living room," Mummy said as she straightened up. "Oh, my poor back!"

Once the storm abated and the floors dried, the paint was flaky and spotted. Mummy solved the problem by painting the floor a lovely, shiny black. While Daddy was out looking for work, she had me sit on the verandah and do my school work while she painted.

We were living here because Daddy couldn't live with his sister, and he thought his dream of a farm might be easier to find in this part of town. But there never seemed to be enough money for him to buy any land to get started. While Mummy and I stayed at home, did lessons, and made the house into a home, he was busy visiting neighbouring farms. It wasn't long before he came home rather excited, saying he had found a farmer whose sow had just had a litter of piglets.

"This might be a good project to start. What do you think, Edie?" Daddy said, his weathered, shiny red face wreathed in smiles, his blue eyes sparkling.

"Maybe you would like to come with me, Janie, and choose a piglet to raise."

"Can I go, Mummy? It will be fun to see the piglets." I asked, even though I saw her mouth tighten, and I knew she wasn't happy with Daddy's idea.

With her steely glare directed at Daddy, she retorted, "Seems like you've decided to go ahead with the farm idea after all?"

Daddy didn't answer, and I looked from one to the other, hoping for a sign that I would still be allowed to go. I knew Daddy would get the pig, regardless of Mummy's attitude, and I knew he had asked me in front of Mummy to soften the tension.

"Go ahead, go with him, Jane. I can't seem to knock any sense into him. Just remember both of you, I am not taking care of a pig, and that's the end of it," she said as she turned and walked away.

Once at the farm, Daddy talked to the owner while I played with the six piglets. They were so cute. There were three white piglets, which looked pink, one all black, and two white with black spots.

"Well, Janie, which one shall we choose?"

"But what about what Mummy said?" I asked worriedly.

"Always the diplomat, eh Janie! It's all right. I've talked the man into keeping the pig at the farm. We'll pay for the upkeep and food until it's time to go market. Mummy will not have to be involved. We can visit anytime. So which one are you going to choose?"

"Let's have one of the white ones, Daddy. Can I call it Charlotte?"

"Whatever you want, Janie," Daddy replied with a happy smile.

Things at home were bright and cheerful at last. Daddy planted seeds in the vegetable patch outside. Mummy, who believed in the saying, "Least said, soonest mended," made bread as usual and sometimes cake for tea. I helped churn fresh butter and did my lessons. Then in the evenings, before I went to sleep, Daddy sat on the bed while Mummy read me a story. It felt like a perfect world.

One afternoon the house was quiet; Daddy was asleep with his legs up on the arms of the planter's chair. I was playing with my kaleidoscope on the verandah when a scream came from the bedroom where Mummy was taking her "five-minute" nap.

"Stay there, Jane!" Daddy shouted as he shot out of his chair and rushed into the bedroom. When Daddy brought Mummy out of the bedroom, she looked pale and shaken. He sat her down in her armchair. "Come and stay by your mother, Jane, while I make her a cup of tea."

"Don't fuss, Clem, don't fuss, I'll be OK. Just deal with the centipede."

Later, Daddy put the dead centipede on a newspaper on the verandah. It was a shiny brown, about eight inches long and over a half-inch wide. Its many legs on either side of its body made me shiver. Even though Daddy said he wasn't superstitious, he took no chances and kept it in full sight. Folklore said that centipedes didn't die until the sun went down.

We were never sure how the centipede got into Mummy's clothes, but it had probably come into the house and crawled onto the bed. Then, attracted by the warmth of her body when she went to lie down, it had crawled up her leg and became trapped by the elastic in her underwear. Although a bite from a centipede can be poisonous, Mummy only suffered a mild irritation of the skin around the bite. But she did remove all the elastic from around the legs of her underwear. She never again laid down to take a nap without checking the bedcovers first.

Daddy and I visited the farm often. Our piglet was growing nicely. It was now weaning and getting fatter. Then disaster struck. I was with

Daddy when the farmer told him the piglet had died. It had got into the cassava water, which was poisonous.

Daddy was angry, calling the farmer an "incompetent fool," and said he wanted his money back. The farmer laughed, and Daddy got mad. He pushed the farmer calling him a "damned thieving nigger."

I was afraid. I had never seen Daddy this angry before, and I sensed it could become a terrible situation.

"Daddy, let's go," I said, my voice wavering.

"Go get in the car, Jane, leave this to me."

"Please, Daddy—"

"Do as you are told, get in the car."

I saw Daddy take another swing at the man, and I leaned on the car horn. It seemed to stop the two men. I saw a woman come out the door and yell something. The two men stared at each other, and then Daddy bent down to pick up his hat. I cringed. The farmer wiped his hands on his pants and told Daddy to get the hell off his land. I leaned on the horn again. Even if it made Daddy mad, I knew he wouldn't hit me. I just wanted both of us to get out of there safely. I was terrified. Daddy got in the car and we drove home in silence.

As we drove back down the driveway to our house, Daddy turned to me and said, "Don't you say anything to your mother, Jane; I'll tell her. You just stay on the verandah and play until we call you."

"Yes, Daddy."

I was relieved he wasn't mad at me but worried about Mummy being angry. I stayed out on the verandah for a long time, until almost dinner time. Despite trying to listen at the door, I couldn't hear them talking. Supper that night was quiet. As soon as Daddy finished eating, he announced in a gruff voice, "I'm going to bed."

"Help me clear the table and do the dishes, Jane, then I'll read you a story before you go to bed." Mummy didn't speak again until I was washed and ready for bed. Then, she said quietly, "Fetch your book; I'll read to you in the living room."

"Can I sit on your lap, then?" I asked hopefully. I wanted her to cuddle me. She looked at me and I thought, Oh no, she's going to tell me I'm too old again.

"I think it will be OK, just this once. Hop up."

Happily, I snuggled up against her while she read *Billy Goat Gruff*, one of my favourites. Mummy was good at bringing stories to life. She made the troll sound scary and the goats adventurous and brave. I loved the world of good conquering evil. I loved the feeling of tense excitement — the feeling of being both scared and safe at the same time.

Mummy kissed me on the forehead and said, "Don't worry about today, Jane, Daddy, will get over it in a day or two. Now go give him a kiss goodnight, then we'll say your prayers, and you can go to sleep."

Mummy sat on my bed while I knelt, hands together to say my prayers, "Gentle Jesus, meek and mild, Look upon a little child...." I always followed my prayers with, "God bless Mummy and Daddy, Brothers and Sisters, Aunties and Uncles, God bless me, and make me a better girl."

None of us went anywhere the next day. Mummy made her wonderful chocolate cake. We played cards, Snakes and Ladders, and read our books, quietly sitting together in the living room. After a couple of days, life seemed back to normal, and Daddy decided to go into town.

"Can I go too? Please, Daddy! Say it's OK, Mummy."

"Sure, dear, I've even got twenty cents for you to spend," Mummy said with a laugh.

I was very excited thinking of all the things I might buy. Did I want an ice cream cone, or a shaved ice with that deep red syrup poured on top, or maybe a toy from Corea's Hardware? I just couldn't make up my mind.

"Come on, Daddy, let's go. I have my shoes on already."

"OK, OK, Janie. Let's get out of here and go shopping."

I looked back through the window as we drove away up the driveway. Mummy stood on the verandah waving, her blue dress with white flowers fluttering in the gentle breeze. She looked happy. I was surprised to hear Daddy murmur, "My beautiful Edie." I'd never heard him say that before. We both waved out of our windows and then closed them against the dust.

Halfway to town, we were forced to a halt by a crowd of angry Black men waving their arms. They circled the car, shouting and banging on the glass. I screamed when I saw a man on Daddy's side raise a cutlass. I closed my eyes tight and put my head down with my hands over my head.

"Please God, send them away; please God, don't let them hurt us," I sobbed quietly. After what seemed forever, I realised that it was quiet outside and the car was moving.

"Are you OK, Daddy?" I asked between my fingers without looking up.

"Yes, Yes, I'm fine. You can look up again. They're all gone."

"I need to go to the store after that shindig." Daddy said, dismissing the horror with a need for a drink.

"Were they after you, Daddy, because you hit that man?"

"I don't think so, Janie, they were just mean, angry Blacks, and we were White and in their way."

"I was so afraid they were going to kill you. Don't do anything silly again, please Daddy! What would Mummy and I do without you?"

"OK, Janie, it's over now. Let's forget about it and go into town and get you an ice cream cone," Daddy said, once again, dismissing the subject and my fears with a sharp tone.

The thought of ice cream at that moment made me feel sick. "Can we go to Corea's first, please? I need to go to the toilet."

Daddy left me with one of the ladies in the store and then went off on his business. What I really wanted was for Daddy to cuddle me, but that didn't happen. I had to bury my fear and get on with my business: go to the toilet and maybe get that ice cream.

Once the secondary terror of wetting myself was relieved, I didn't mind being left in the store. There were so many toys to play with. There were lots of fancy electronic cars and walking, talking dolls, all of which came from America.

I didn't know it at the time, but part of Daddy's business was to look for another house for us to live in.

In our new home, Daddy would become very ill and I would sink further into myself and my fears.

House on the Rocks

We moved a couple of weeks later into another house. After the house on the hill, this house seemed like a rich haven. Yet by the time we left, it felt like a release from prison.

The house was isolated. It sat at the end of a hard-packed mud lane, which probably became a river in the rainy season. We never lived there long enough to know what would happen when it rained. The setting was beautiful, with the house built out over large rocks looking into the Calliaqua Bay.

The large picture windows of the living room looked over a sheer drop into the deep blue-green water. It was the only part of the house filled with light. Looking inland, one saw a semicircle of coral reef, the shallower blue water of Calliaqua Bay, dotted with small fishing boats pulled up on the white sandy beach.

I loved to sit in Mummy's chair near the large windows and look down. I'd imagine I was much older and I could high dive off the rocks into the crystal water below, with the gracefulness of a bird, and cut the water with barely a ripple. It was my magical dream! When Mummy sat there, I sometimes saw tears in her eyes as she stared out of the window, her book lying unread in her lap. I asked her what she thought about it. She replied, "I read, so I can't think."

I guessed she was sad and worried because Daddy was sick with DDT poisoning.

Because we were so far from town and Daddy, the only one who drove, was in bed, I had to stay home from school until he was better. Mummy was busy taking care of Daddy, and I had to find my own entertainment and not trouble her with demands for attention.

In the beginning, I would take my blue teddy bear and wander down to the beach, where I would try to rescue the little red fish that the fishermen threw out of their catch. I would put them in a bowl of water and try to keep them alive. The fish never lasted long before they went belly up, and I had to throw them away.

On other days, I would go into the wooded area on the other side of the mud lane. One time, I left my blue teddy stuck in the fork of a tree while I picked wild cherries. When I went to retrieve him, he was gone. Instead, wrapped around the tree branches, was a long brown snake. I fell, jumped, and ran from the tree into the house, screaming for Mummy. She couldn't come because she was busy taking care of Daddy.

I was angry and felt rejected. I found Mummy in the kitchen. She was mixing some white powder into a glass. "Is that for Daddy? Can I take it to him?"

"No, I'm sorry, Jane, you mustn't disturb Daddy."

"I only want to say hello."

"No, Jane, you can't."

I didn't understand all the feelings rushing around in my head. There was no one for me to talk to or play with. I couldn't even keep the baby fish alive. I just wanted Daddy to get well again. He had sprayed many crops before; why did he get sick now? I didn't know anyone; we couldn't go anywhere. I couldn't even go to school.

When Mummy left the room, I tried to pick up Wong, who was asleep on the chair, but he didn't want to be picked up and struggled to get away. In my frustration and anger, I bit him. "I hate everyone! I hate you too, you silly cat!" I cried and ran out of the house.

I ran outside and down to the sandy beach below the house. I sat against an old log, washed up on the beach, and cried until there were no tears left. I felt that I had no one, not even my teddy bear. I sat there until I saw a red crab scurrying across the dry sand. I picked up a shell, and I threw it at the crab. Then I saw many more red crabs in and around the trees further back from the beach. I threw another shell: the crabs disappeared into their holes in the sandy dirt beneath the trees at once. I turned away, "Even they don't want to play with me." But when I looked back a few minutes later, they were back. Maybe — I thought, and threw another shell. "Yes!" They ran for their holes again; now I had a game to play. I was the conquering knight, laying claim to the land. They would be mine to control.

Sometime later, I heard Mummy calling me.

"I'm coming," I answered, jumping up and sending the crabs scurrying for their holes again.

"I'm sorry I can't spend any time with you, Jane. You must understand, Daddy is very sick, and I need to take care of him."

"I'm sorry, Mummy, I'll do better tomorrow."

"Good girl. Go wash your hands and let's have some supper, and then you must go to bed."

"Yes, Mummy. Can you read a story to me tonight?"

"I will try, as long as Daddy doesn't need me."

That night we had tripe and onions cooked in milk. It was a favourite dinner of mine, soft, tasty, and slipped easily down my throat.

"I made you chocolate pudding as a treat."

"Oh yummy. Can I have some sugar over the top?"

Mummy passed me the sugar bowl and milk jug with a smile. I poured the milk into my bowl, making a brown island in the middle, and sprinkled the golden brown sugar on top.

"Smooth and chocolaty," I said with satisfaction. "Mummy, I can read my book in bed if you are busy. I just want Daddy to get better."

Mummy came in to hear my prayers and tucked me into bed with a kiss. "Sleep tight, and don't read for long. Tomorrow is another day."

When I woke up Mummy, was already up and making breakfast.

"I've left your porridge on the table, Jane. Come and eat it before it gets cold."

Although I was supposed to sit at the table and eat, I put the milk and sugar on my porridge, took my special Bunnikin's bowl to Mummy's chair, and sat down. I watched the sea and wished I could go into Daddy's bedroom. I wanted to see him, make sure he still knew who I was.

Outside, the sky was clear and blue. The only clouds were high in the heavens, and light beams streamed through the window across the floor like dancing rainbows. Today was going to be a good day. I was going to be a pirate and bring home lots of treasure. I knew we didn't have much money, even though Mummy never said anything about being poor. I was going to wander along the shore in search of a smuggler's cove, a place where I knew the pirates hid their treasure. I had read that they anchored beyond the reef and came ashore undetected in their small boats.

"Jane!" Mummy's voice brought me back to reality with a bump.

"Run down to the farm and bring some milk and a little butter: my purse is on the table."

55

"Yes, Mummy, I'll get dressed immediately." I was determined not to cause her any bother today.

The walk to the farm and back wasn't far, and on the way I found a great stick. One end was thick, the other smooth and flat like the blade of a sword. Now, I could be a pirate and find that hidden treasure. Once back at the house, I put the milk and butter in the fridge. I put on my swimsuit and called out to Mummy. "I'll be on the beach; your purse is on the table."

I played happily up and down the beach for hours that day. I climbed trees and swung from the branches. I crawled into spaces where the trees had grown together to make a tight nest of branches. I waved my sword around in the air and cried "Aha" and "Ho, ho, me hearties." I was alone but enjoying myself. I loved the feeling of freedom when I was happy. When I was tired of playing, I lay down on my back in the shallow warm waters and felt the sun beat down on my body.

Before going back indoors that day, I returned to my game with the red crabs. A few of the shells and twigs I had thrown at the crabs yesterday had gone down the holes. I was sorry now, feeling I might have hurt the crabs.

To my amazement, the crabs weren't hurt. They had pushed the twigs and shells out of their holes; I had a new game to play. To make it more interesting, I went into the dining room and took a few of Mummy's teaspoons and even a small knife, which I dropped slowly into a hole. I loved that all the foreign objects were re-deposited back on the surface the next day.

About six months later, Daddy was finally getting better. At first, he walked at the speed of a snail, but he slowly improved. We began going into town again. Daddy started working at the Corea's Hardware Store on Bay Street, and Mummy got a job as the bookkeeper at the Blue Lagoon Hotel on Front Street.

It wasn't long before we moved back to Arnos Vale, this time to live in the middle bungalow, where Mummy and Daddy had once lived with their first family. It felt like life would finally be better. I could visit Aunty Gussie in the big house, visit Conrad, and play in the gardens. I also started at the elementary school in town.

The only thing I missed from the previous house was lying in the shallow warm water and those crafty red crabs.

Schools: An Education for Life

When I look back, I went to a different school every two years or less of my school life.

I started at the age of four and a half at the Rectory School in Bathsheba, Barbados, where Captain Tom, the retired sea captain, was my teacher. By the time I was five, I was in a church school with what today would be called an abusive disciplinary code. The Anglican Church ran my new school, but it was not a convent. There were both nuns and civilian teachers.

We still lived in the rectory, and for a short while, I caught a bus to school.

What I remember most was the pleasure of travelling by myself and getting my own ticket from the conductor. He wore a wide black leather strap in a diagonal cross over his uniform with a black machine attached on his front. The conductor turned a dial on the side and cranked the handle to print out a ticket. He would occasionally give me an extra string of used tickets to play with. He wasn't amused when I refused to get on or off the bus one morning, demanding that the driver wait for a friend running to catch the bus.

This new school had a large airy classroom with widely spaced wooden desks and chairs. We used wooden frames with various learning activities to do in each. There was one with buttons and buttonholes. It had wide coarse fabric ribbons on either side of the frame with large buttons on one side, and a corresponding buttonhole on the other side. Another frame had shoelaces and ribbons in threes for braiding.

If we did not already know how to tie our shoes, do up and undo buttons in different types of materials, or weave ribbons in a crosspatch fashion. This is how we learnt. We also learnt to brush and braid hair. The goal was to master the art of dressing quickly without assistance, which we needed to do for sports activities. Most of these I already knew how to do. Mummy taught me to be independent and dress and brush my own hair. Tying my shoes was difficult, and the practise helped.

I had to be responsible for my "sand shoes" (soft canvas shoes) needed for sports activities. I carried my shoes to school every day, along with a separate white shirt and blue shorts, in a cloth bag with my name embroidered on it. The bag hung on a wooden peg along with my lunch box and raincoat. There were repercussions for losing or misplacing your belongings.

I was a quiet child. I learnt quickly, watching the misfortunes of other children. The school required that a child made every effort to excel; there was no room for the slacker or the defiant. The teachers were often cruel towards Black children, especially the White teachers. They would grab a child by the ear, smack them over the head, or taunt them for being incompetent. I remember much older girls than me crying and wailing for some misdemeanour they had committed.

Colouring within the parameters of a picture was another of our learning skills. We had large sheets of stiff paper printed with a simple design: a chick, cat, dog, duck, or pig. The drawings had a thick black outline. We were never to colour outside the lines.

One incident left a permanent mark on my life. A little girl went over the lines. I do not know whether what she did next was out of fear or defiance, but she committed the worst sin of all; she tore up the card and threw it away! The teacher boxed her ears, picked her up under the arms and took her away. For a long time, I could still hear her screams from the small dark cloakroom at the back of the classroom, where they locked her in solitary confinement. I have no other memories of that school. I do not remember how long she was shut up in the room, I do not remember if I ever saw her again, but the incident left deep scars and behaviour traits in my emotional makeup about people of authority.

I loved my uniform in that school. It was a blue cotton dress with puffed sleeves, a white Peter Pan collar, and a blue bonnet. Even after we left the rectory, I continued at that school until we moved to Montserrat in September 1956, not long after my seventh birthday.

School in Monserrat was another church school. This time an Anglican convent for girls. The nuns who ran the school were strict but kind; everyone loved them. They never raised their voices, were gentle and loving, and had a smile for every child.

It was the first time I loved school and enjoyed working hard at my lessons; my record cards showed the results of good work. But what I remember most was our playtime. I was only at that school for a year before we moved again — this time to St. Vincent.

I was nervous and shy when I entered the Kingstown Preparatory School, a government-run school, for the first time. I'd missed almost a year of school since we arrived in St. Vincent. On my second day, as I entered the wide-open gates, I was approached by a group of kids.

"Hey you, new girl, we picked these pretty berries for you."

I smiled, "Thank you," and popped one into my mouth. My face turned bright red, tears ran down my face, and my mouth burned. The pretty berries, 'bird peppers,' were the hottest berries that grew on the island.

Bullying was rampant and being an acutely shy and emotional White child in an almost all-Black school, I was an easy target. One morning, I had only just walked into school when the bullies surrounded me in the hall chanting, "A hurricane's coming, a hurricane's coming."

I was so overwrought by the intimidation that I threw up and had to leave school. I made my way to the Blue Lagoon Hotel, where Mummy worked. Of course, she told me that I was a silly girl.

"Hurricanes are just a lot more wind and rain than usual. You know that."

"But they make me afraid, and the kids at school make fun of me."

"Well, this is what we'll do. You can stay with me today, as long as you are quiet and don't bother anyone in their rooms."

"Can I have lunch here too? In the dining room?"

"We can do that, but tomorrow when you go to school you are to thank the children. Tell them you had a wonderful day. They'll be envious that you had a special day out of school, and I think they will not mention hurricanes again."

I wasn't keen on the idea of approaching those children again, but I did have a wonderful time in the hotel that day. I was able to walk away the next time the bullies teased me about hurricanes.

"You can't make me afraid anymore!"

These incidents made me reticent to open up to other children, but I did make a couple of friends. The first was Kaye, whom I used to watch, mesmerized by her ability to hold her breath until she almost passed out. We became best friends for a while after I refused to join in with a group of White girls who "sent her to Coventry" which meant the girls deliberately excluded Kaye from their social group, refusing to even acknowledge her presence in the room. Being friends with Kaye was easy: her body vibrated with energy and her eyes sparkled in a round face surrounded by a mass of long black curls. We were opposites in looks but burned with the same fire for adventure.

We spent a wonderful weekend at my home: built a camp, caught fish with a bent hook, made a fire, and roasted the fish for our lunch. We finished with cookies left in Mummy's cookie jar. We splashed through the river and climbed trees along the banks, searching for the ripest and sweetest hog plums. Kaye fell into a hornet's nest and got stung several times, yet surfaced laughing! I do not remember her coming to stay again, but our friendship at the time remains a strong memory. Being with her was the best time I had while at that school.

Pearl was my second friend. We were odd-ball kids who didn't fit into the world of other kids. She lived with her uncle, "old man DeFreitas." He was a man known for his odd character. After his death, many years later, he was buried upright in a large white cross on a rocky island of Indian Bay.

Pearl and I spent our lunchtimes together under the school, digging for what I remember her calling "bac bac turtles": small beetles that spiralled down into the ground. I watched her, captivated by her pale skin and long silver-blonde hair hanging around her face, almost touching the ground. She always pulled her skirt tight and tucked it between her knees, that nearly touched her chin. Pearl would dig into the tiny holes in the dry sandy dirt to capture the creatures. I wasn't interested in the bac bac turtles, but I was fascinated by the sand falling back into the holes like inverted volcanos as the "turtles" spiralled downwards. I would help her by holding the jar into which she put the beetles. I would shake it occasionally to keep the beetles at the bottom. It was too creepy to have them touch my skin. Pearl did not last that year in school. I heard she'd had run away from old man De Freitas and gone to America; she was only twelve years old.

Corporal punishment was still practised in colonial schools in the late fifties and sixties. Our teachers used a leather strap; it was a two-foot piece of raw-hide leather, three inches wide. In my last year in elementary school, a kid put a realistic plastic centipede in the class register. When the teacher opened it to take registration (roll call), her screams brought the headmaster to the class. No one came forward to accept responsibility. The boys had to line up behind each other in the classroom, and each received two lashes from the strap; girls were excluded. The only time I received the strap seemed most unfair. I misheard the teacher's request for an adverb and I wrote a verb instead. The error cost me one lash with the strap on the left hand; I was the only left-handed child in the class. I felt I could see those marks for years afterward.

But the worst incident that happened in that school was the day the headmistress called an unscheduled assembly. I was about ten and a half years old. They were always held on Thursdays, and it was only Monday morning.

Daddy had dropped me off at school that day, so I was early. I walked quickly from the road to the school, hoping not to run into any of my tormentors. I noticed an eerie silence plus an unusual sound immediately after I walked in the door. The sound was chairs being put out for an assembly.

"Don't dawdle in the hallway, child. Go quickly to your classroom," the headmistress called after me.

I slid into my seat in the second row, in front of Bertie, the only other white child in my classroom. Bertie was mean and horrid to all the children. He yanked my ponytail, which brought tears to my eyes. After registration, the class lined up and moved silently down the hall to the assembly point, where a raised platform had been set up with a row of straight chairs for the teachers and an armchair in the centre for our headmistress.

I trembled in my seat, afraid that something terrible had happened. All was quiet; pupils were aware of the wrath of our headmistress. The piano struck a chord as the teachers filed onto the stage. We all stood and sang the national anthem. "God Save our Gracious Queen".

Once the rustling of chairs had quieted, the headmistress entered the stage, her hand grasping the wrist of little seven-year-old Terris Leroy. The headmistress's face appeared fierce and angry, while Terris dragged his feet and looked at the floor. I felt sorry for little Terris; he was a sweet little boy, a few years younger than me. He always had a happy smile on his face. What had he done to upset the headmistress, and so early on a Monday morning?

"This boy is a criminal; he shot his baby sister with his father's gun."

I remember the gasps of horror from the children sitting in that assembly, plus the stern faces of the teachers on the stage. I remember the tears running down my face. I felt like a criminal, just being there.

How could Terris be a criminal? He was only a little boy. I looked up and saw silent tears running down his face.

The local paper said he had accidentally shot his sister when he picked up his father's gun; it was still loaded with scatter-shot. I felt that to have been shamed in front of the whole school was a crime. The injustice of the moment affected me greatly.

The Middle Bungalow

Living in the middle bungalow at Arnos Vale was a paradise for a child who loved to play adventure games. Just outside the front door of the bungalow was a large mango tree. It was a marvellous climbing tree. My little legs could barely straddle the lower branches when we first moved into the house.

Beyond the tree on a sunny slope was a large cottage garden which contained a variety of fruit and vegetables. Conrad had women come in daily to care for the area. There were pineapples, always sweet and juicy. The tomatoes were bigger than my fist. There were aubergines, which I only liked fried, yams, which were white and fluffy with a nutty flavour, sweet potatoes, which I loved, the flesh cooked and scooped out mixed with butter, salt and pepper, and put back into the skins. There were shallots, lettuce, taro or dasheen, and corn. Eddoes grew well, but it was a vegetable I didn't like very much because, like okras, they were slimy when cooked. There were also christophines or chayote, a small pale green pear-shaped vegetable, with a clean, bland taste. I liked the flat almond tasting seed in the centre best.

When I wasn't in school, I was free to go anywhere and eat anything. I feasted off the fruit of the garden and the forest. I'd enjoy sitting on the bottom saddle-shaped branches, squeezing and softening the large Julie mangos. I'd bite a small hole in the top and suck out the juice; it was truly delicious.

Every morning I collected the fallen mammea apples from the ground around the two trees that grew on either side of the driveway. I'd take them into the kitchen and ask the cook to peel the hard skin off the dark orange fruit and slice it up. The taste was interesting; it was a cross between a slightly ripe mango, an apricot, and a splash of sweet lemon.

Soursop had to be picked when very soft and ripe. The fruit had a pulpy, white, fibrous texture, which minus the black seeds, made delicious ice cream when blended and frozen. I liked eating fresh custard apples; they also made great ice cream or a delightful, creamy drink. On hot afternoons, we enjoyed sitting on the verandah, drinking sorrel. It had a beautiful red crystal colour and made a wonderful light and refreshing drink.

One of my favourite toys from Corea's Hardware was a battery-run miniature juicer. Across from my bedroom window, there was a Surinam cherry tree; it had small knobby fruit. I'd take a bowl from the kitchen, climb the tree, pick the ripe cherries, come back down, and put about six cherries in the juicer. It made a terrible noise with the stones still in the fruit, but I loved the few teaspoons of liquid it produced.

Beyond the cherry tree, the woods were dark and mysterious. I loved wandering through this area, the rich, spicy smell of the dark undergrowth. A huge nutmeg tree grew in the woods. I'd break the fruit open, take off the mace, the deep red lacy flesh covering the hard seed, and take them home for our cook.

I didn't like the immense iguanas but was fascinated by their dragon-like appearance, especially the dewlap, which puffed up when they were startled. I respected their place in the dark woods, as long as they didn't jump on me. The local Black people caught and killed the iguanas for food; it was said that the meat tasted like chicken. I was told that when my older brother and sisters (Mummy's first family), lived in the bungalow, the area was a beautiful Savannah.

The bungalow had a verandah that ran the width of the front and left side of the building. The front of the building looked out through the mango tree, over the cottage garden, and right down to Arnos Vale House. The three bedrooms were on the right side of the house. Each room led into the other through an opening in the dividing wall. The wall stopped short of the ceiling by about two feet, allowing for ventilation. Daddy's bedroom faced the verandah, Mummy's in the middle, and mine was at the back of the house. My room also had a doorway into the bathroom. It was like having my own bathroom. Of course, Mummy and Daddy shared it too.

One night in the fog of a bad dream, I rolled out of bed, fumbled my way around the bottom of my bed, through the open door, along the edge of the bath, bumped into the kitchen wall and grille window, turned around and took five steps and sat down. Not complicated, even without lights. We never used lights after we were in bed. I always believed it was so we didn't disturb anyone else, but maybe it was to cut down on the cost of electricity; Mummy was always frugal.

Returning to bed that night was not so simple. I could not reverse the technique I used to enter. I bumped into the walls in every direction except the door into the hall. Finally, I realised that I could walk down the hallway, go through Daddy's and then Mummy's rooms and find my bed from there. It was a relief to return to bed.

Although Daddy didn't seem to like his sister, Auntie Gussie, I found her fascinating; her clothes, the house, and especially her dogs. She was always buying new dogs, most of whom unfortunately never lasted long. Two of her dogs did live for a long time; they were Reddy, her old cocker spaniel and Tessa, her boxer, which was Auntie Gussie's last dog, while I was still living on St. Vincent.

I loved playing with these two dogs while we lived in the bungalow; Reddy was caramel red in colour, soft and quiet, with beautiful eyes and a happy smile. Tessa was a purebred boxer of medium height with a sleek brown body. She had soft ears, a short stubby tail, and a grin that spread from ear to ear. I loved making her excited, her red tongue and stub of a tail moving really fast as her body whipped nose to tail. Her behaviour made me laugh so hard.

Auntie's American bulldog and pit bull mix had a massive head and body with short, squat legs. Conrad had trouble controlling him because he was so heavy. To me, this dog was ugly and scary. I heard rumours that he was the killer of the sheep on the estate. At first, Auntie Gussie insisted that it couldn't be her animal. One night, the dog was observed leaping from an out-jutting rock onto a sheep's back, clinging onto it until the animal was dead.

"Expensive god-damn hobby," Daddy said when he heard what had happened.

Auntie Gussie's macaw, Dan, was already quite old by the time I was a little girl. I loved to watch him swooping around the central gardens at Arnos Vale House. He loved to cause trouble; he used mimicry to continuously upset the servants. Dan would pace the fence and taunt our cook until she threw something at him. Then he would start screeching, bobbing his head, and cussing her royally.

Dan was afraid of only one thing, a tiny bird called a flycatcher, who nested in the top branches of the mango tree. If Dan tried to land in the mango tree, the bird flew angrily at the macaw's head. Dan would screech, "Oh Gad, she mash me," sounding just like our cook when she was hurt. His most troubling behaviour was to fly alongside cars at eye level with the drivers, causing them to leave the road and go into the ditch. It was Conrad's job to catch Dan and bring him home again.

Daddy didn't seem happy living at the bungalow or working for Auntie Gussie at Corea Hardware, and Mummy was quiet and sad, but there was one advantage for me. Daddy could bring me a special doll or a mechanical toy for free once in a while. I loved whizzing the remote control cars around our long corridors. There was one toy I especially remember; it was a brightly coloured promenade on which tiny figures twirled and danced along a central groove. I kept winding it up, watching the tin people turn and spin until it finally broke.

Christmas at the bungalow was quiet that year. Our beloved cat, Wong, had disappeared. Mummy and I spent hours looking everywhere for him. I cried for days. Mummy thought Wong was stolen by one of the workmen who had been around the estate that week, but no one had any information. We had given up hope until one day, six weeks later, I saw him dragging himself slowly up the driveway. I ran to pick him up, hugging his poor, thin body close. We were so happy to have him back as we were preparing to move again, this time to Calliaqua. Wong never went far from the house after that. We decided that he must have escaped from those who had stolen him and walked all the way back home to us.

Sunningdale

Daddy was finally happy, living his dream of having his own plantation farm. Daddy named our new home Sunningdale, after a small village in the Southeast of England. It had an emotional significance for him. I liked the name, but he never explained why he chose the name. The house was a stone building in the middle of an acre of land a mile or two up the Calliaqua Valley and nestled on the flatlands, below the Mesopotamia Hills.

Daddy grew black-eyed peas and big fat tomatoes in the upper field, which I loved. The times when Daddy gave me a tomato fresh off the vine, I was always thrilled. I'd take it indoors, cut a deep cross into the firm red flesh, sprinkle it with salt and pepper, and then, holding it together with two hands, I would take it outside to eat. The juice would drip down my hands, off my elbows, and into the dusty soil.

The lower half of the field ran down to the river. A large grove of timber bamboo grew along one edge. In this area, Daddy planned where to put his passion fruit vines. He eventually bottled the juice and exported it to Fortnum and Mason in England.

First, he had to prepare the land, dig irrigation ditches, and plant seeds. I cut the timber bamboo to make an eight-foot-high trellis for the vines. I felt grown-up cutting the bamboo because I used a machete. Sometimes, I'd have to climb the bamboo to free it from the clump. One time I slipped, falling a breath away from the machete. I was lucky because I only grazed my knee. Daddy paid me twenty-five cents from the ice money for every perfect pole I cut. He had the only ice box in the area and people came to buy ice from him. I saved the money in Daddy's used shaving stick holders, which were just the right size, until I had enough to buy magazines about horses and ballet. I loved the grace and beauty of the girls, but it was the adventures that the girls had that really appealed to me.

It was in this house I felt the most settled. The four years we lived there seemed like a lifetime. When Daddy couldn't afford help, or he'd sacked the Black man working for him, I also helped out by picking the tomatoes and the black-eye peas. If there was a storm warning, I went up on the roof to securely hammer in all the nails.

"Just hammer those nails in tight," Daddy would say. "Don't want to lose the roof."

If the nails weren't secure, it was goodbye roof, a financial disaster for Daddy and a lot of hard work for Mummy. I was light and agile, and I could crawl over the galvanized roofing quickly.

Mummy, wouldn't let Daddy go on the roof. "He might fall off," she'd say.

When we first moved into Sunningdale, we had no bathroom, only a smelly outhouse. Daddy employed Ryan, a Black man who lived on the neighbouring field, to dig a cesspit and build a new bathroom. It took nine months, during which time we had a lot of rain. I remember the shallow pit filling with water and the brilliant blue, red, and green dragonflies that darted across it in dazzling arcs of colours. I was fascinated by their ability to hover over the water with fast-beating wings. I also loved splashing the water up into the air and watching for rainbows as it fell back into the hole.

Until we had our new bathroom, Mummy and Daddy sponged bathed in the kitchen after I had gone to bed. I was allowed an old tin tub in the garden. I'd put on my blue seersucker swimsuit and play for hours in the tepid water. It was much better than sponge bathing!

"Make sure you wash down as far as possible and up as far as possible," Mummy would say.

I once asked, "What about possible?" but her only reply was a light clout on the side of my head for being cheeky.

I loathed the outhouse. The smell of the Jeyes fluid disinfectant was awful, but it was the cockroaches that petrified me. They were large, brown, and made crunching noises when they crawled over the floor and walls. The worst part was when they dropped from the ceiling. I used a Tilley lamp to see the stepping stones to the outhouse at night. I loved jumping from one to the next, but once I reached the door, I hesitated to enter; the cockroaches came out at night!

When Ryan finished the cesspit and covered it over, I was sad. The beautiful dragonflies no longer flew, dipping and rising over the water in glistening arcs of blue and green. But the grass grew long and lush. Daddy seemed very excited one day when I came home from school.

"I want to show you something, Janie," he said. "What do you think about this?" showing me the home he had built for the chickens.

"Oh! Are we going to get chickens?"

"Yes, maybe a few ducks too. You can help Mummy take care of them, especially collecting the eggs when they start laying."

The chicks rapidly grew from fluffy yellow balls of chirpiness into Leghorn chickens. I adored their tiny peeps and cheeps and loved to watch them huddle under the lamp at night. I would rush home from school every day to see how much they had grown. We had to separate them as they grew because of feather pecking.

I learnt that chickens establish a social hierarchy from an early age by pecking each other. Roosters rank the highest and the weakest chickens the lowest. Once an open wound or blood is visible on a bird, a vicious habit of cannibalism spreads rapidly.

I overheard Daddy and Mummy talking about the various reasons chickens turn to cannibalism. In the case of our chickens, it was the slow feathering of the tail feathers.

It was a traumatic few weeks! Daddy painted their tail ends with purple ointment: Gentian violet. He used it for many things, including the time he had ringworm on his legs. Mummy also cooked up special food to improve the chicken's diet, which seemed to help.

I was frightened, angry, and frustrated, feeling sure they would kill themselves. I continually got into the cage to separate them. I even turned the hose on the chickens, but nothing really seemed to work.

One chicken was badly pecked and bleeding. Mummy put it in a cardboard box under the kitchen sink. "Removing this one will help. I don't expect she will survive the night."

The next day, quite early on a Saturday morning, I heard a squawk followed by a scream. Soonie, the girl from across the road, had arrived to start cleaning the floors before we got up and she had found the chicken sitting on the table in the kitchen. I named the chicken Belinda. She turned out to be a survivor, a force of nature, an expert acrobat, and also a bird-brain comedian! She would fly up into the air with a sharp squawk and come down on the kitchen table, often right in the middle of Mummy's bread making. This would result in both Mummy and I chasing Belinda around the house, Mummy shaking a tea cloth at her and me trying to catch her. As my hands closed around her body, Belinda squawked, flew up in the air, and came down on my head.

One time, in the middle of her antics, Belinda landed on the hot stove. That caused a great kerfuffle and cacophony of noise as we ran around the tiny kitchen trying to catch her. Eventually, she flew out the door, landed near the other chickens, flew back up in the air with a loud squawk, and then laid an egg! That was the end of Belinda living in the box under the kitchen sink.

Although Mummy continued to prepare rice and vegetables for the chickens once a day, they were great foragers, finding most of their food, especially in the grass over the cesspit. The chickens liked to roost at night in the orange and avocado trees behind the outhouse.

After school, it was my job to find the eggs. I enjoyed searching amongst the dark green spinach leaves by the side of the house or under the orange tree. I often found an egg tucked under a clump of flowers in Mummy's garden. Occasionally, I disturbed a chicken nesting. It would fly up in the air and rush around the yard, squawking and flapping its wings. It was such a funny sight. I found it hilarious to watch Wong, our cat, stalking the chickens. He'd throw out a paw and jump in the air, pretending to catch them, although he never really got close enough to touch them.

I ate quite a variety of eggs. Daddy liked the duck eggs best because they were so big. I thought they were a bit strong-tasting. But on rare occasions, I'd have one. It was fun to have one egg fill my plate. I usually preferred chicken eggs. Our Leghorn chickens produced lovely white eggs with dark yellow yolks. In addition to fresh eggs, we also had bacon, sausage, and sometimes liver with our breakfast.

When Belinda was destined for the cooking pot, I was upset because I thought we would keep her forever. She had been my pet. I could always recognise her in amongst the rest.

For the second time in my life, I ran away that day, hiding out in the woods and riverbed, too angry and afraid to come home. Daddy laughed at me when I finally came home just as it was starting to get dark. "Just in time for dinner, eh?"

"Chickens are raised to eat. Fact of life my dear," Mummy said. "Now go wash up and sit down at the table."

It was hard to eat any dinner that day.

One of my favourite games was to take Mummy's large mirror off the wall. I'd hold with my hands either side of the frame, and walk, looking down into the mirror. I was good at walking around the house, but outside was more difficult. I loved the thrill and sensation of this upside-down world and never stumbled.

When this was no longer exciting, I changed my game to reading while walking. The idea was never to take my eyes off the page as I walked. I would even climb up into our avocado tree while reading. I used one hand to climb and the other to hold the book. I never had an accident, despite the many warnings from Mummy. I also wanted to understand what it would be like to be blind. I would walk around the house, dress, and even come to the table for dinner with my eyes shut.

I loved running in and out of the house, watching Mummy in her pretty blue dress. One of her favourites had tiny white daisies with yellow centres. On her feet, she wore white leather sandals, which Daddy cleaned and whitened every evening before he went to bed. She lit up the grey walls of the lean-to kitchen.

Once a week, Mummy baked bread. When it was cooked, she would stand in the kitchen doorway and call out, "Coo-ee, come and get it." On those days, Daddy and I would come in from the fields and sit down to a large slice of soft, warm bread with crunchy edges, slathered with homemade butter. I'd have a glass of cool, fresh milk, and Daddy would have a cup of milky coffee. Daddy's extraordinary baby blue eyes would twinkle as he looked at me, "Not bad, eh?"

One day when I was around twelve, I was sitting in the car, waiting for Daddy to come back from the store. I had taken Mummy's lipstick from her dresser earlier that day because I decided I wanted to experiment with makeup. It was the old-fashioned beetle juice red and had a funny, waxy, earthy smell. I applied the lipstick without looking in the mirror, just the way Mummy did. As I pressed my lips together, I glanced up and saw two women pointing and laughing at me. I was so embarrassed, wishing that the car could absorb me into its thin walls and unpadded seats. I shrank down below the window, my heart beat wildly and tears welled in my eyes. When I recovered enough to raise my head and look into the reversing mirror, I recognised my twelve-year-old face, but it looked like a two-year-old had been in charge of the lipstick. I was mortified. It was another action I never forgot.

One year I built a house with coconut fronds. It looked like a teepee. Daddy wired four bamboo poles together for me while I dug small holes to keep them stable in the ground. Together, we lifted the poles into the holes and I lashed the fronds to the framework using string, which I hid between the leaves. I wanted to sleep in my teepee, but although we lived in safe times, Mummy did not think it was a good idea. Instead, I made a table and three chairs from scrap plywood I found around the garden, swept out the dirt floor, and invited Mummy and Daddy for tea.

Wong, always a proud and haughty cat, was the first to enter the new domain. Bingo, my dog, forgetting his manners, tried to push his way in. Wong gave him a painfully sharp reminder by dropping his claws with accurate precision on the end of Bingo's nose! His plight was so funny that Mummy, Daddy and I laughed until we ached.

Another day, I caught my first crayfish with a bent pin. I cooked it in a tin over an open fire. I didn't really enjoy eating it; the noise it made in the pan while being boiled was most off-putting. But catching the crayfish was great fun.

Our washing was done by Soonie. She took everything down to the river and used a wooden washboard and slapped and scrubbed it until it was clean. The white clothing was dipped in a bucket of bluing as a final rinse to keep it white. This was mostly cotton underwear and Daddy's shirts. At the time, he wore only white ones. Afterward, Soonie wrung the water out of the clothes, brought them back to the house, and hung them on the clothes line to dry. Our clothes faded and wore thin very quickly with this method.

Mummy always washed delicate things in the kitchen sink and hung them out to dry. Soonie ironed all the clothes the next day. I liked to mix the starch she used on Daddy's shirt collars, sheets, handkerchiefs, and my school shirt.

Mountain Water

The man who came to the house that morning had black leathery skin. His name was Thomas. He wore an old blue shirt with cut-off sleeves and khaki pants, tied at the waist with coarse rope. His dog, called Billie, was a black and white border collie mongrel mix. He had alert eyes, a mouth open in a wide grin, and a very happily wagging tail. I opened the front door and immediately started playing with Billie. I wanted a dog of my own. Thomas often stopped by to chat with Mummy on his way up to the mountain. She said that the next time he came by I could go with him.

Thomas called though the house to Mummy, "Mornin' Missus. Canna take ya childe up moun'ain with me this mornin'? It be lovely toda!" Thomas had a small red and white checkered bundle tied to a stick, which he carried over his shoulder. "I'zz got the vittles, Missus."

I was already wearing brown shorts and a blue-flowered blouse with a Peter Pan collar. I hastily shoved my feet into a pair of old leather-soled Clark's sandals and we were off on an exciting adventure by nine-thirty on a summer morning. We walked together, not talking much, in the already bright sunshine. Billie trotted quietly at Thomas' side.

At the far end of our field, we passed a run-down shack on a piece of land bordering ours. Ryan lived there with his woman, Delilah, and their son, Willie. Ryan worked for Daddy when he wasn't too drunk. The air around their house smelled of pigs rooting in the dirt outback. Ryan's woman squatted out front by an open fire, feeding and singing a bawdy song to the baby.

Further on, we passed my best friend, Gloria's, home. She had a brother, Noel, who I thought was special because he was born on Christmas Day. Gloria also had an older brother, who I didn't really know, and two younger sisters. I also remember her mother because she made her Christmas cake and pudding with twelve eggs and mixed it together in a metal bathtub. They kept chickens, ducks, and goats for food and milk. I liked going to their house to play because it was different from my home.

Thomas, Billie and I walked on for about an hour before we stopped outside a run-down, shanty kind of building with a long wooden bench on the outside. A few very old men sat there smoking pipes. I could see a long counter through the door. Behind the door, there were shelves stacked with canned goods.

I had strayed this far from home once before, and a woman brought out some bread and cheese for me to eat. Her throaty laugh and demand that I stay outside made me nervous at first, but the bread and cheese were different from anything I had ever had at home. It was so good. It was Island food; it tasted warm and sweet like the air itself, salty like fresh mountain water, and the mysteries that lay behind their black, black eyes.

Now, with Thomas, I went inside. It was dark and musty. An old, rusty Frigidaire hummed in the corner. Inside were ice cream, salty yellow butter, and the bright orange tangy cheese made by the women of the hills.

The woman's rough laugh broke the silence. "What ye be goin' wid dem White gal To'mas? She be too young for the likes of ye."

"Hush ye mouth, woman, and gimme two bread and cheese for the journey."

I stayed close to Thomas and watched while she took two bread rolls from under the counter. She sliced them in half with a large knife and smothered them with the yellow butter and a chunk of cheese before wrapping them up in brown paper.

"Tank ye Sadie, I'll be seeing ye later," Thomas said.

Sadie laughed with her deep voice, "Sure ye will, me man, sure ye will."

"Come child, let be goin'. Let us git back into the clean air."

The rocky, dusty road was no longer accessible to vehicles and I wondered if the native people used donkeys up in the mountains. The few people I saw in this part of the island seemed different, older, craggier, and wore unusual clothes.

After leaving the shanty shop, the trees grew denser and denser, forming a heavy canopy overhead, making our surroundings dark and mysterious as we walked. It was nice to feel Billie walking next to me during this time.

Eventually, we left the rocky ravine and moved out into the warm sunshine. We climbed slowly across and up the grassy slope. Trees were sparse now but large and wide. My favourite was the tamarind tree, with its lacy leaves and brown sweet-sour fruit hanging down from the branches like many-waisted worms. There were a few large, grass-hugging boulders scattered across the meadow.

We stopped by an enormous boulder, and Thomas unfolded the red and white checkered cloth and took out two small glasses and a large bone, which he threw to Billie. He placed the bread and cheese on the cotton cloth and told me to follow him. On the other side of the boulder was a tiny trickle of water which Thomas let fall into the glass, "Now drink," he said, handing me the glass.

"It's fizzy!" I exclaimed.*

"Real mountain water," Thomas replied.

"Us'll eat now."

We sat on the grass together: a White child, an old Black man, and his dog, eating and looking way off into the distant valley below, at peace with ourselves and the world.

Footnote:
* A remote mineral spring in the Mesopotamia Valley, where the water filters through underground mineral-rich volcanic rocks, absorbing minerals such as chloride, carbon and sulfur, giving the spa water its distinctive bubbly taste.

Puppy Love

About a year after moving from the middle bungalow to Sunningdale Calliaqua, Daddy came home with a box for me.

"Thought you might like one of Reddy and Tessa's puppies. Auntie Gussie is giving them away."

"Let me see, let me see," I squealed with delight.

"Open it up then, Janie" he said with a smile.

I hadn't had a dog since I was three years old. I had loved rolling around on the grass or floor, holding onto one end of Pedro's bone; at least, that is the story Mummy always told me.

"Can I hold him, please, Daddy?"

"Of course, he's yours," Daddy said. "Your Auntie Gussie wanted to get rid of him. She furious that her prize bitch...."

"Clem! Mind your language."

"Well... Tessa and Reddy had a litter and she let me take this little fellow."

"Why don't you call him Bingo?" Mummy said. "You are always singing that song."

"B.I.N.G.O. B.I.N.G.O. Bingo was his name O." I sang as I ran outside with the puppy barking at my feet. Bingo was smooth-haired with small soft ears like Tessa, the boxer, but he didn't have a docked tail. Bingo's face had the proportions and shape of Reddy's face but with a black, wet nose.

My friends laughed at me for calling him Bingo, but I didn't care. I was a proud owner and protector. While he was still a puppy, I would pick him up and carry him whenever we had to pass another dog. As he grew, he became my protector too. He'd stay close to my side and bark or growl at other dogs if they came too close. One time the situation was reversed. A much older dog attacked Bingo, and without thinking, I rushed into the fight, shouting, "Don't you hurt my dog," giving the attacking dog a hard whack on the nose.

When Bingo was fully grown, he would catch his long tail in his mouth and spin around in circles when excited. He went everywhere I did, except to school. On those days, I'd change out of my uniform when I got home, and we'd go play; usually, hide and seek. I would hide, and Bingo would come and find me.

I didn't know much about dogs and their sense of smell back then, but if I had, I would have thought him the cleverest dog in the world because he would pretend he couldn't find me. He'd run in and out of the rooms giving short sharp barks as if to say, 'Where are you,' until I called out again and again. Finally, he would come rushing to my hiding spot, usually behind the clothes in my wardrobe. We'd both be so excited that the cupboard would shake as he tried to get inside. Once, it nearly fell over, but I jumped out in time and pushed it back against the wall!

That's when Mummy would call out from the kitchen, "Will you two get out of the cupboard and go play outside."

As Bingo grew, we were always together on evenings, weekends, and holidays. We were often gone all day. Mummy and Daddy never seemed to worry where I went or how long I was out as long I was home for dinner by five. Mummy kept a big cowbell by the back door and when it was time for me to come home, she would ring it. The bell would echo through the hills, and the local Black people passed on the sound of the bell from person to person until finally, it reached my ears.

"Yer mudder be calling yer chide."

Bingo was never on a lead, but he usually stayed close. He might chase a wild cat or other small creature for a short time, but he would quickly return if I called him. There were no property barriers where I lived, and wandering through the hills, was a blissful and happy time. If people were friendly to Bingo, he would wag his tail joyously. But if he growled and the hair stood up on the back of his neck, it was time to move on quickly. There were areas considered more dangerous for White children to roam; the Blacks of these areas were considered "free thinkers," not having the "healthy respect" for Whites that the colonial way of life expected from them. But I wasn't afraid. I had Bingo with me, and I liked being amongst some of them. They were usually kind people who called me "Whitey." Being a naive, innocent child at the time, I believed it was an endearment!

I never took lunch but ate off the land. I could climb any tree and eat its fruit: the soft sweet guavas and tart brown tamarinds, with their shiny seeds from which the locals made beautiful necklaces. The lovely, red-skinned plumrose, with its pleasant rose fragrance, white cotton-wool flesh with a mixture of pear, apple, and plum flavour, with a distinct aftertaste of rose petals. Yellow, thin-skinned hog plums, when I could find them, were another pleasure. Bingo would lie beneath the trees for as long as I wanted to pick and eat. I also loved akees, a fruit similar to lychee. I'd crack their thin brown shell and suck the slightly tart jelly-like flesh off the black stone. While out in the hills, Bingo and I drank water from tiny springs running through mountain rocks.

I went home with brown teeth, purple-stained hands, arms, and face if I hadn't been able to wash them under a standpipe in one of the small villages. There would often be a long line of women and children carrying pans or buckets to collect water. As we approached and joined the line, some of the women would move aside and encourage me to go ahead and drink. I always thanked them and sometimes played with the children before moving on.

Bingo and I would sometimes only go as far as the ravine and cross the river to the other side. There was an old Java plum tree growing against the wall of the mental asylum. High up in the tree, I would lie along the thick branches, hidden by the green foliage, eating the tart bottle-shaped fruit. Its blue-purple juice stained my teeth and hands. I liked to watch the "poor crazy people" wandering aimlessly around the courtyard below, muttering to themselves. They seemed so sad, angry even. I wanted to call out and say, "Bingo and I will be your friend." But I never did because I heard many tales of crimes committed by the crazies shut up in this terrible place.

There were times when I would go to the old tree, lonely and sad. Sitting there, I would find my peace. I would climb up the tree with all the pain and angst of a thirteen-year-old and climb down happy. I went home knowing I was loved and free to roam wherever I wanted.

Ticks were common in the Caribbean. When Daddy got them on his legs, he used the lit end of his cigarette to burn them off. He said, "It makes it release the head without leaving the claws embedded in my skin."

When Bingo got them, I preferred using the sharp-nosed tweezers that Mummy suggested. I was afraid to use Daddy's cigarette in case I burned him, and I hated the smell of the smoke. When I found bumps under Bingo's smooth hair, I would sit on the front steps of our house with a can of kerosene or Jay's fluid; both smelt nauseating. Putting Bingo between my legs, I'd apply the tweezers between the tick's head and Bingo's skin and pull. Deprived of a meal of healthy blood, I'd watch the tick's legs waving frantically in the air before dropping it into the can of liquid. I always prayed I wouldn't squeeze too hard and have Bingo's blood spurt over my hands.

A Hard Lesson

I loved living in our little house on Glen Road, Calliaqua. I built dams for swimming holes, used bent pins to go fishing, built a tent from bamboo poles and coconut fronds, and one year, advanced to a wattle house. I wove thin bamboo poles in and out of upright poles stuck in the ground. It had two rooms with a connecting door, windows, and a roof. My only companion, most of the time, was Bingo.

On this particular day, "I had the devil in me," Mummy said. I wore my silky yellow petticoat, which now had been lengthened with a cream, lacy edge around the armhole and hem. Around my waist, I had tied a wide, bright red, shiny ribbon.

"I'm a bad fairy," I told Mummy as I danced around her as she sat at the dining room table typing.

"All right, dear, but don't bother me; I'm trying to write a letter to Lorna."

"Ha-ha, bare toes," I cried as I crawled around under the table, tickling her toes poking out of her white Clark sandals.

Mummy twitched her feet around and I imagined her smiling just a little, perhaps even telling Lorna what I was doing. I ran around the house, in and out of all the bedroom doors, and jumped on Daddy's lap while he was reading *The Vincentian*, the Island newspaper.

"Oomph! You flattened my tummy," Daddy said, followed by, "why don't you go outside and play Janie," as he ruffled my hair.

"No, no, I can't do that. I am a bad fairy, up to all kinds of mischievous tricks," I laughed. "I'll turn the radio off and on again, I'll tickle your toes and undo your shoes, I'll flicker the lights and hide your matches, I'll make you laugh, I'll make you mad. Will you chase me now, or chase me later?"

"OK, OK, that's enough now; off you go and bother your mother," he said, his blue eyes sparkling.

I kissed Daddy's cheek, knocked his glasses askew, and jumped off his lap, scattering his paper all over the floor. I ran around the house again, through Daddy's bedroom, then mine, in the middle, then Mummy's, then outside to the bathroom, back in through the kitchen and back to Mummy, busy at the typewriter. I pulled a hairpin from her wispy bun.

"Now you've gone and done it!" Mummy said, her voice thundering. She placed her hands on either side of the typewriter, pushing herself up, and scraping her chair back across the floor.

I wasn't afraid because Mummy had a way of sounding gruff while her whole face lit up. She was only playing at being angry. I screamed excitedly and ran through the living room, planning to run out of the front door and around the house and come in the back door. Instead, I ran straight through the closed front door.

Breaking glass exploded all around me as I came to a halt just short of the steps into the garden, still laughing. But then I saw blood pouring onto the ground.

Mummy was out of her chair in seconds. She grabbed a towel from the kitchen and wrapped it around my arm, and Daddy was already starting the car.

"Where are we going, Mummy?" I asked tearfully.

"To the doctor's house. Just be still and quiet, dear."

I wondered what his name was and where he lived, but I didn't ask. It was nice to cuddle up against Mummy.

Our car at the time was a very primitive grey Citroën 2CV, which Anne, my older sister, had bought in France and shipped as a present for Daddy. The seats were bouncy with removable box springs with loose grey covers. Mummy didn't like being a passenger because Daddy wasn't a careful driver. She always sat with her fingers crossed and her eyes shut, mouthing silent prayers. Today, she only had the fingers of her left hand crossed because she had her right arm around my waist.

There were no posted speed limits on the island and Daddy drove fast. We didn't go all the way into town; Daddy turned off before we reached the airport and drove up into the Mesopotamia Hills. It was somewhere I had never been before. Daddy drove for a while until we came to a large rundown house. He got out of the car and knocked more than once. A lady opened and spoke to Daddy, and then he beckoned Mummy and me to come.

81

"Thank God, the doctor's at home," Mummy said quietly. "Come on, Jane, let's get this over with."

Mummy and Daddy stayed in the anteroom while the doctor took me into a room that looked like an ornately furnished living room. He sat me down on a chair and put my elbow on the table facing him. "OK, let's take a look."

I flinched as the doctor took the towel off my right arm. The bone glistened white through the flesh of a big, triangle gash.

"What's your name, kid? How did you do this?" The doctor said in a slurry voice. His breath smelt terrible.

"Jane. I went through our front door."

"You'll have to sit very still while I put a stitch in it."

His wife brought in some things and laid them out on the table: a roll of white bandaging, a length of black, shiny thread, which looked like the stuff I tied to my bent pins for fishing, a can, and a strange-looking metal object that turned out to be the needle.

I started to cry, "Can my Mummy be with me?"

"No, no. You are a big girl. It's better if your parents stay outside," the doctor said.

I watched him put some stiff black thread into a needle in the middle of the metal contraption. While the doctor's wife was attempting and failing to spray my arm with something cold from the can, the doctor put the metal object against my arm and pushed the large needle into my skin. I screamed and screamed.

I do not know how long it really took the doctor to put one stitch into my forearm, but it seemed forever. When he finished, I stopped screaming. He called my father to come in and pick me up.

I heard Daddy say, "You damned bastard!"

"Where's Mummy?"

"Out in the car, waiting. Let's get out of here, Janie. I'm sorry it was so bad."

"I'm all right now," I said. "But I never want to go back there. You won't ever take me back there, will you, Daddy?"

"Hush, Janie. We are going home now."

I noticed that my yellow petticoat and the towel were covered with blood as I got into the car next to Mummy.

"We can get Soonie to wash the blood out of your petticoat," Mummy said.

"I don't ever want to wear it again. Please, Mummy, can we throw it away?"

"Go slowly on the way home, Clem."

When we reached Calliaqua, Daddy asked if I would like an ice cream. I nodded happily. I heard Mummy sigh audibly when Daddy returned with my ice cream cone. He may have had a drink in the store, but he did not come out with a bottle bulging out of his pants pocket.

I learnt two life lessons that day which have lasted the rest of my life: don't trust a drunk, and don't ever play at tormenting someone; it can lead to a comeuppance not expected.

Arnos Vale and Auntie Gussie

After we moved to Calliaqua, I occasionally visited Auntie Gussie at Arnos Vale House, known locally as "the house of a hundred windows." It was a large plantation house with many rooms upstairs, some of which were rarely used. It had a beautiful sweeping mahogany staircase in the hallway leading from the front of the house to the bedrooms. I loved to slide down the bannisters when Auntie Gussie was upstairs resting and couldn't hear me. It was great fun.

On one side of the stairway was the morning room, where I practised the piano and had tea in the afternoon with my aunt. On the other side of the stairway was the dining room with a large ornate mahogany table, polished to a high shine in which I could see my face. We sometimes had breakfast at the table, served by Gertrude; it was close to the kitchen, and she was getting too old to climb the stairs in the early mornings. Usually, it was reserved for larger family gatherings. All other meals were served on trays, either upstairs in the playroom or in our bedrooms; Auntie retired early in the evening and had supper in her room.

Off the dining room was a small kitchen where Gertrude made the meals. The shower room was originally a pantry. I enjoyed wandering through the rooms of Arnos Vale. I was in awe of the grand furniture and wall hangings. I could wander freely as long as I was careful, didn't touch anything, and didn't disturb Auntie Gussie.

One of my favourite books at the time was about a little girl called Sadie, who found a secret passage in her house. Sadie followed it to a different world outside and got lost. She fell asleep in a fairy ring and became a changeling. I would amuse myself for hours, tapping along the carved and ornate walls of the rooms, checking for secret doorways, looking for a way into the fairy realm of magic and mystery.

Auntie Gussie collected the most beautiful books I had ever seen; amongst others, a complete collection of the Victorian Encyclopedia

Britannica. I became engrossed when I read, travelling the world through stories. Auntie Gussie's call for me to come for tea would often go unanswered until she came looking for me.

My favourite places outside were the servants' quarters and the washhouse. Both places were cut out of the bedrock on which the house stood. Conrad and Gertrude, Auntie Gussie's manservant and housemaid, lived in tiny concrete rooms underneath the kitchen and outside the washhouse. My uncle, Fred, brought Conrad and Gertrude to the plantation when they were young teenagers; they took care of my cousins when they were babies, the house, the property, and the grounds.

Gertrude was a private person and kept her room locked, never inviting me in. Conrad was different, quiet but always smiling, and never too busy to talk to me about anything I cared to ask. He rarely saw his family because they lived in the north of the island. Conrad cooked all his meals outside his room on a round open-fired stove. Gertrude, I believe, ate her meals in the kitchen.

The washhouse was a large stone-floored room with three deep sinks down the middle of the floor, with an old washboard in each of them. There were two kinds: one, a grooved wooden board, and the other, a fluted metal scrubber in a wooden frame, made from either tin or zinc.*

The room was underground so the only light came through narrow slits in the wall, located at the ceiling level inside but were at the ground level outside. Two young girls came out from town once a week, and under Gertrude's orders, they boiled, washed, scrubbed, blued, put the clothes through the wringer, and hung them up to dry. Gertrude would talk to me in the washroom, telling me all about the art of washing. But I was not allowed to put my hands into the bluing solution; it would stain my hands.

One day while I was visiting the washhouse, I noticed that the large wooden door to the storage area at the back was open. I often tried to look into this section from the outside, lying on the concrete walkway that ran the length of the backside of the house and imagine all kinds of mysteries waiting for me to discover, but I never saw anything other than cobwebs draping the windows.

I always wanted to explore "the under-house," as Gertrude called it, but she'd always stopped me, "Mistress be most displeased if I am letting you do that."

Now I had a chance. I sneaked in quietly while Gertrude wasn't looking and quickly became involved in imagined treasures of another time and place. It became darker and darker as I ventured further into the back of the storage room. Fortunately, I always carried a torch (flashlight) with me. It made the shapes and shadows lengthen, and I imagined them as grotesque and sinister characters.

I became lost in a world of make-believe and fantasy. I imagined the ornately carved wooden chests that stood against the wall to be filled with treasure. I was Aladdin, opening the chests and finding gold and jewels, looking but not touching. I imagined unrolling the old musty carpets stacked against the wall and flying away over the seas and mountains. I journeyed to India and the Taj Mahal, the Savannahs, and the deserts of Africa — even the grim, foggy streets of London. In the middle of my breath-taking fantasies, I suddenly saw it! It was almost completely hidden behind boxes. It was just what I wanted.

I ran back out into the washhouse. "Gertrude, Gertrude, can I have a wet rag, please?" I called excitedly. "I found a bicycle. Do you think Auntie will let me have it?"

"Laud loves us, child; where have you been?"

"Having adventures. Gertrude, please, can I have a rag?"

"Can't keep my eye on you all day," she said with a smile. "You'd better take a bath before you go into yer aunt. Mistress ain't gonna be pleased with ya covered in dust and cobwebs. Go bring that bike out here, and I'll lock that door up again, and I'll ask Conrad to clean it for ya. Now, you shoo upstairs and get clean up."

Later, while having afternoon tea in the morning room, I broached the subject of the bike.

"Auntie, I found a green bicycle in the back of the washroom. Who does it belong to?"

"To whom, child."

"Sorry, Auntie, to whom does the bicycle belong?"

Auntie Gussie's eyes took on a dreamy, faraway look. She told me about her son, Archie and daughter, Joan and how they had enjoyed their bicycles when they were young. Finally, she asked what I was waiting to hear.

"Would you like to have it?"

"Oh, yes, please, Auntie." I cried, jumping up out of my chair but promptly sat down again, remembering we were in the morning room.

Footnote:
* In 1868, the *New York Times* called washboards "a great American invention."

87

An Old Green Bicycle

"Oh, yes, please, Auntie," I said, jumping up out of my chair, but very quickly sat down again, ashamed for we were "in the morning room."

One day, not long after I had discovered the bicycle in Auntie Gussie's dusty cellar, Daddy came home with the bicycle hanging unceremoniously out of the Citroën, I was so happy. I wanted to get on it immediately and pedal away into the sunset. I was such a romantic dreamer in those days.

"Oh no, wait a minute, my girl. First I will overhaul it, clean it and make sure it is all working, and you are going to help me so that you can do it the next time."

We cleared the living floor, which fortunately was concrete!

"Make sure you roll that carpet up, Clem, and don't spill any oil on the floor," Mummy said, handing us an old worn bed sheet to lay down first. "You need to pay attention to your father, Janie; he'll do a good job."

Daddy handed me some special bike spanners and showed me how to fit them over the nuts and start undoing them. He also gave me the best advice I ever had. We created a template on the floor for putting every part of the bicycle back together correctly.

Daddy spent the better part of two or three days going over everything with me. He didn't go out into the fields or down the road to the shop and come back drunk. We took the bike apart, every bolt, screw and rod, and laid the parts on either side of the bicycle frame until it was left standing bare in the middle of the living room. I cleaned and oiled the pieces and then put it all back together again by myself.

"Let's check the brakes and you will be good to go," Daddy said.

I felt so proud of what I had done.

Mummy made bread as usual, and gave us big, warm slices slathered with home-churned butter. It was delicious. Occasionally, we danced a jig of "Hands, Knees and Bumps a Daisy" around the living room and out into the kitchen, and Daddy gave Mummy a kiss on the back of her neck and twirled her around. She shook him off with a laugh as usual, but it was such fun.

Learning to ride the bicycle was a big hurdle for me. I could steer well, but I just couldn't seem to balance, mainly because I was afraid of falling off onto the stony road. It took various friends, and Daddy when he could, running alongside me, before I finally mastered the art.

My friend, Noel, was running alongside the bike, talking to me. "Look straight ahead, Jane, and don't stop pedalling."

I was so focused on keeping my head up, keeping the handlebars straight, and pedalling hard to stay on the bicycle, I failed to realise that Noel had let go of the bike some fifty yards back on the road. When I discovered he wasn't there, I promptly fell off. By the time I had untangled myself, Noel caught up to where I was.

"Why'd you let go of me, you meanie?"

"You did it, didn't you? Just get back on. I'll give you another push and I bet you manage to ride this time."

Noel steadied the bicycle while I put my foot through the frame and hoisted myself up onto the saddle. "Ok, push me off."

I was off and away, wobbling a little at first, but I did not fall off. I was so excited. I was finally able to balance, pedal, and steer.

My world opened up. I could go farther and faster than ever before. A bit more practise and Mummy might let me ride to school. I would avoid the awful embarrassment of having to stand in the road and hail down a passing car to take me to school, or have the bus driver refuse to let me on the bus because Daddy hadn't paid the monthly fare. I could go to the Aquatic Club without waiting for Daddy to take me. I could visit friends in town.

By the end of the summer, I had persuaded Mummy to let me ride to school. I learnt to put my skirt over the saddle so the pleats wouldn't be crumpled when I reached school. The nuns would punish me if I arrived at school in a wrinkled state.

"Bye Mummy," I shouted that first morning as I rode off to school on my new green bicycle. Down the stony road I went, from my house to the post office and the main road. I turned right and kept on up the hill to the Aquatic Club and down to Indian Bay. I always looked for the big white cross where old man DeFreitas wanted to be buried.* The idea of being buried upright in a large hollow cross filled me with awe. Then it was downhill to the airstrip, which was just a dirt track across the road with no barriers to prevent traffic from crossing when a plane took off or landed. I was wary cycling across the airstrip and kept my eyes on the airport, always looking in case a plane took off. I often wondered what would happen if I were halfway across and a plane appeared.

After that, it was a long slow climb, past the cigarette factory, and on up Arnos Vale Hill, past the old house where Aunty Gussie lived, and the glorious moment when I reached the top. I always stood a while and looked down over the bay. I could see the ships in the harbour off to the left below and Kingstown to the right. I would free-wheel down the long curving road past the high school and the elementary school where I used to go before I needed to start peddling again. I cycled past friends' houses, along Back Street, past the cinema, around the Anglican Church, and arrived at St Joseph's Convent just in time for school to begin.

Thank goodness Mummy had no reservations in letting me ride a bicycle in public or wearing trousers or shorts if I was going to the beach. A few people had grumbled to Mummy that it was very unladylike for me to ride a bicycle; they suggested I would develop muscles in all the wrong places.

The old green bicycle I had seen in Auntie Gussie's dusty old cellar became my best friend for the next few years before I left the island. It allowed me the freedom to go places independently, a powerful experience.

It felt so good that I allowed my friends Noel and Gloria to persuade me to go with them to the next Carnival. I would be thirteen. It was 1963 and the era of the Carnival Queen Celebrations. I knew a few of the girls, friends of friends, who became carnival queens.

"Come with us to the Carnival, Jane," Noel said. "Gloria, Bev, and I are going into town with Daddy, you can ride with us."

"I'm not sure I can," I said quietly, "I'll ask Mummy."

I was hoping to hide behind her refusal. I was still deathly afraid of the devil stealing my soul, but didn't want to tell my friends about my fear. Noel followed right behind me when I went into the house.

"I'll look after Jane, Mrs. Moller," he said,

"You make sure you do," was all she said before turning away.

Mummy was like that. She felt everybody should be trusted, and one had to live through your fears and come out on the other side. She also believed that everyone, even a young child, should experience for themselves the right and wrong of every action.

I remember holding onto Noel's hand tightly once we were in town and refusing to stand in the street. Noel found us a place to watch the parade from an upstairs window.

Footnote:
* One of St. Vincent's first entrepreneurs, Sylvester Gonslaves DeFreitas was buried on Dove Island in a standing position within a huge white cross. He was a man of exceptional vision and an outstanding businessman. His main concern was transforming the way of life in St. Vincent. His pleasures were women; he apparently fathered as many as 52 children, the first ten with his wife. His vice was smoking; an average of 200 a day! He made elaborate plans for his death, securing a 99-year lease of Dove Island off the coast of Indian Bay. He had his coffin built years before he passed, trying it out for comfort before he was satisfied.

St Joseph's Convent

I transferred from the elementary school to the two-roomed Roman Catholic convent in the early 1960s, just before I turned twelve. St. Joseph's Convent was a fee-paying school, but my sister Anne was paying, and she considered I would do better there than going to the all-girls high school. My good friend, Kaye, went to the high school, and we lost touch after that.

I only really remember two of our nuns: Mother Theresa, the principal, and Mother Immaculata. Mother Theresa was small in stature and had a beautiful face with a soft, gentle smile. She taught us sewing, oversaw the lunchroom and organised the annual school fair. Mother Immaculata was a tall, loud, Irish woman who overemphasized the "H" in every word. I couldn't understand what she was reading. Because of it, I failed at spelling and dictation every week. Mother Immaculata was also in charge of the scriptures. She gave us a chapter of the New Testament to learn every night and expected us to write it out in full the next day. To receive a good mark, we couldn't make any mistakes. It was a lot to memorize. She punished mistakes with a rap on the knuckles with a ruler for every wrongly spelt word or misplaced punctuation. We all thought she was a tyrant.

Cricket was a popular sport. In 1963, my second year at the convent, the West Indies won the cricket match over England. One of the girls had a radio and did not contain her excitement. Unfortunately, we were in the middle of the sacred chanting of the Rosary. For the rest of that year, we all stood outside in the sun for the hour-long Rosary. If a child fainted, they were left where they fell until we finished the prayer. I learnt resilience quickly.

I also learnt how to cheat when I couldn't memorize the whole chapter of scripture. All the pupils in my class did. We kept our scripture books open inside our desks, raising the lid occasionally to make sure we were replicating it correctly.

Mother Immaculata was hard on me for being left-handed. She insisted that I kept my book straight and rapped my knuckles if I didn't. The problem was, we all wrote with liquid ink pens, and I smudged my writing if I didn't keep my paper at an angle. I experimented at home and learnt to write with my left hand up and over the top of the paper, "like a crab," Daddy always said if he watched me doing my homework.

Our lunchroom was an unlit open basement with long benches and tables where all the girls gathered for the midday hour. The room was ideally situated for the nuns to spy on us. It was underneath the sewing room, where the nuns ate their lunch. They could easily hear if we weren't following the rules or the chatter was unseemly.

We were supposed to be young ladies, and the hot midday sun was dangerous for our complexions. Getting hot and sweaty was frowned upon. The older girls congregated around the toilets in the back, out of sight of the nuns, to smoke. I thought it was stupid and likely to get one into trouble. I preferred to read while eating.

It's funny how some memories intricately affect our lives. There was a girl named Pauline, I still remember from that lunchroom. We weren't particularly friendly because she was part of the group who ostracised Kaye in elementary school.

I remember Pauline's creamy white skin, long blonde hair, blue eyes, and doll-like mouth. During lunch one day, she lifted her skirt to show a large bandage above the knee. We all gathered around, as children do, to watch a gory revelation. She had used her father's cutthroat razor to shave her legs. She unwound the bandages and showed us the deep wound, which was swollen and had a lot of stitches. It was a life lesson that always stayed with me. I never shaved my legs; I only used creams as a teenager and at nineteen gave up removing the hair on my legs entirely.

I never did well at sewing at the convent. Despite my best efforts, I could never manage to make the metal footplate of the treadle where my foot rested, move the needle forward. I would treadle the plate slowly and carefully until the machine needle began to move forward. As I stitched faster, I would lose control. The treadle would careen backwards, wrecking my stitching. Eventually, I learnt to sew on Mummy's sewing machine, an early electric Nechi. But my humiliation of being unable to use the school machines was great. I resented Mummy not having an old-fashioned machine on which I could practise.

When the Catholic boys school was built across the road from us, the nuns had a six-foot wall built across the front of our school to prevent us from eying each other across the street. When dismissed from class, I ran the gauntlet of boys who hid behind the wall and threw crackerjacks; tiny packets of twisted and folded paper filled with gunpowder, which jumped and sparked in numerous unknown directions once lit.

I was a shy and non-aggressive child who suffered from repetitive dreams of violence. I was terrified by the jumping, sparking crackerjacks. To avoid showing my fear, I relied on romantic stories. I pretended I was a heroine escaping the dungeon guards as I ran along the street, away from the laughing tormenters.

Once home, I would be quick to strip off my starched blue pleated skirt and white calico blouse with its Peter Pan collar and puff sleeves. Once changed, I was ready to play with Bingo until dinnertime.

Trouble on the Streets

Before I had a bicycle, getting to school was a painful embarrassment. If Mummy and Daddy were going into town, they would order a taxi, and I could go with them, but they only went into town once a week and not always on a weekday. I had to find other ways of getting a ride into school because it was too far to walk. When Daddy remembered, he would pay the bus driver a fee for the month. Then, I would walk to the end of our stone road and catch the bus into town.

The bus came from up north, quite a few miles away. By the time it reached Calliaqua, it was packed with people going to market, who carried big baskets of vegetables and fruit, and live animals going to the slaughterhouse. I was always uncomfortable with being the only White child on board. If I was lucky, an older woman would be kind and offer me a space next to her, protecting me from the jeers and taunts of the working men and women.

The women were often the worst. I was always afraid on those rides. It was excruciating if Daddy either forgot, spent too much on rum, or there just wasn't any money to pay the fare. There was a deep-seated belief system that being White equalled money, stability, and of course, a car. We had none of those.

One day, while on the bus, a man suddenly collapsed, his body jerking and writhing with what looked like foam coming out of his clenched teeth. The bus driver stopped and a couple of the passengers carried the man out of the bus and laid him down on the road. I was terrified, believing the devil had taken possession of the man. I had never seen anyone have an epileptic seizure before. I really hated taking the crowded, noisy bus.

The alternative to the bus was even more humiliating. I had to cadge rides from people driving past my road, going into town. I learnt quickly to recognise my friends' parents' cars and stand near the edge of the road with the hope that they would be going slowly enough to see me and stop. If I thought I'd be late, which was frowned upon by the nuns and punished with extra work at lunchtime, I raised my head in defiance, as Mummy taught me, and stepped out into the road and waved down a passing car.

I never begged or pleaded with Mummy not to take the bus. I was relieved when Daddy set up a routine with one of the shopkeepers on Back Street to pick me up and return me to the post office on the corner of our stony road every school day. I enjoyed the stress-free ride to and from school until one afternoon. A shop window was broken and they couldn't leave the store. I was too shy to ask the shopkeeper to call a taxi for me so I waited and didn't get home until almost dark.

I was upset and in tears because, for the first time, Mummy didn't listen to me. She was very angry with me. She had called the police when I didn't come home at the usual time, which made me ashamed. I believed police only came to the house when there was a crime. I went to bed hungry and cried myself to sleep. I didn't understand why I was wrong. I felt the injustice of the situation deeply.

The absolute worst situation I experienced getting to school was with a taxi cab driver who was awful to me. I knew that Mummy and Daddy were going into town that day, but for some reason, they still insisted I walk to the end of the road and cadge a ride. I was very upset. Why were Mummy and Daddy doing this to me? I was determined not to get a ride. I planned to wait for Mummy and Daddy to come down the road and then run out and say I hadn't been able to get a ride.

It didn't happen that way. I ran out into the street, but Mummy and Daddy didn't see me, but the driver did. I sprinted after the car screaming, "Stop, don't leave me." I was so sure that at least Mummy would see me and tell the driver to stop. When the cab driver eventually slowed enough for me to catch up, they weren't surprised or upset. I never understood why they weren't sympathetic. An added insult came later that day. Traumatised by the event, I became sick and was unable to continue at school. I didn't know where Mummy and Daddy were, so a taxi driver was called to take me home; it was the same man from the morning's trauma. He laughed at me, calling me a stupid, spoilt White bitch. I believe my anger and distrust of people may have begun during this time.

In another street incident, I was standing around in the backyard of the small general store in Calliaqua. I was waiting, hoping, Daddy would come out of the store and walk home with me. On rare occasions, he did. It was always wonderful to get the chance to talk and listen to his dreams. As I bent to inspect something on the ground, I saw a tall Black man dressed in baggy white trousers and a long jacket over a white cotton vest come out of the back door. He noticed me and immediately started taunting me and making lewd jokes about Daddy. I picked up the nearest stone I could hold in my hand, stood up, and threw it at the man with force, hitting him just below the knee cap. I heard his shout of pain and curses, but I was off running before he could catch me.

After I left school, it was quicker and easier to walk up Sion Hill pushing my bicycle than to cycle slowly up the long wide street that curved around the town. It also meant I could stop at the corner house and read the Marvel comics belonging to my friend Rose's brother. I loved the fantastic world inside those pages.

I had recently made a beautiful pink embroidery anglaise dress for my niece, Jeanne-Marie, in Trinidad. It had been packaged and sent via one of Auntie Gussie's boats, but it had never arrived. One day, while walking up the hill, I saw a pale brown-skinned man with large black freckles on his face. I often had nightmares about being chased, and this man looked like the person from my dream who had taken the parcel. This was the first time a dream appeared to be true.

I stared at the man, my mouth falling open, my eyes suddenly wide and terrified. "You! It was you, wasn't it?" I stammered. He started to move towards me but turned and hurried away in the opposite direction. Tears ran down my face. I ran up the hill as fast as possible, never once looking back. I never went back on that road again until the day of Hurricane Flora. From then on, I cycled slowly up Richmond Hill until I reached the top of Sion Hill. Then, I enjoyed the long freewheeling of Dorchester Hill, past Arnos Vale and down to the flatlands of the airport.

Another time, walking from school along Back Street, I saw two Black men attacking each other with long curved cutlasses. The sun bounced off the raised blades, and thick, deep red blood dripped off one man's arm onto the black tar street and sizzled in the heat. For a split second, I stood paralyzed with fear, then ran.

Traveling Alone

The morning was exciting. I was getting ready to travel to Trinidad to visit Anne for the summer holidays. Mummy and I usually went to Trinidad together, but not this year. I was travelling alone because Mummy said she was too busy to go. I had my own passport and a small tin suitcase with my name painted in white.

I rode with Daddy alone, in his old French Citroën. It was like a toy car; even I could drive it, and I wasn't quite nine years old.

The dock was full of people milling around; White people waiting for the rowboat to take them out to the banana boat, or the Geest liner, as Anne would later inform me. There were customs officials wearing khaki shorts, jackets with white shirts and socks, their black truncheons by their sides. They marched smartly across the dockyard, issuing orders and tallying the crates of bananas being shipped abroad. There were also Black men and women carrying large hands of green bananas on their heads. The women wore colourful clothes, and the men wore khaki pants, no shirts, and tatty straw hats.

Their rich, throaty voices carried as they sang, "Com' Mr Tally man, tally me banana."

Wearing my new, shiny, milk coffee coloured pants and a white blouse with a Peter Pan collar, I carried a new straw boater in one hand and a wicker basket over my arm.

Daddy carried my suitcase in one hand and held my hand with the other. Waiting alongside the dock was a small rowboat with four passengers already sitting waiting. One sat in the bow, one aft, and two on the forward slatted seat. A large Black man sat waiting for more passengers to board.

"Yuh goin' tuh da boat boss?" He tipped his hat at me.

Daddy just nodded and handed him my suitcase. He stepped into the rocking rowboat with one foot, held out his hands and lifted me into the boat before stepping off the dock with the other foot. We both sat on the aft slatted seat in front of the boatman. I used my hat as a shield to watch the boatman as he rowed us out to the ship. His bare arms were shiny and bulged and quivered as he pulled on the oars. I lost interest after a while and trailed my hand in the cool, dark blue-black water streaked with rainbow colours.

The ship had a platform at the water level with a long, steep metal staircase raising from the water to the deck above. The boatman pulled right up to the base. Holding the painter in one hand, he jumped onto the platform, grabbed the railing, and helped the passengers off the dinghy and onto the platform.

I felt small, walking up those steep metal stairs, and held on tightly to the rails on either side as I walked up. I felt much better once I stood on the deck. Young Black boys were diving for coins, thrown into the water by passengers. They looked like tadpoles from the height of the deck.

Daddy took me through to the bridge to meet the skipper. He was a British man with bushy whiskers and wore a white uniform. Daddy gave me a quick hug and a pat on the head. "Be good, Janie, Make sure you do as Anne tells you now."

"Yes, I will, Daddy."

I stood alone on the deck of the ship, watching Daddy leave. I saw he still had my passport in his shirt pocket; he had forgotten to give it to me. I waved and shouted, but Daddy obviously thought I was saying goodbye and waved back. A horn blast filled the air, drowning my voice. I saw Daddy turn and wave once more.

Oh no, I thought, I'm now alone on the ship without a passport. I was a little scared, but I knew I could do it. I had been preparing for this trip alone for a few months. I leaned against the rail for a moment, watching the Black boys still diving for pennies. The water was crystal clear blue-green, threaded with shiny rainbow streaks. I knew that it was oil from the engines of the Geest ships.

In the years before this one, I travelled with Mummy on the *Lady Angela*, one of Aunty Gussie's boats. It was a drifter fishing boat with a deep hold. We were usually her only passengers. Mummy and I sat on the forward deck in the afternoon and early evening; Mummy knitted, and I read. When the sun went down, we curled up together in the captain's tiny berth-hutch on the deck and went to sleep. We never woke up until the sun rose and the coast of Trinidad was visible.

Once we were out of the harbour, I went to the skipper, who was in charge of me for the next twenty-four hours until we reached Trinidad, and told him Daddy had forgotten to give me my passport.

The ship was my playground. I spent my time getting into as many places as I could. If the men weren't too busy, they were happy to answer any questions I asked. I liked the bridge the best because it was out of the wind. I could see the waves rolling under the ship and watch the Grenadine Islands as we passed. I "kept my eyes peeled," as Mummy would say, hoping to see flying fish leaping out of the water.

The engine room was fascinating, with all the moving parts working in synchronization. But the noise was loud, and the smell of diesel was nauseating. I felt the same sickness in the pit of my stomach in the galley; it was so tiny that when I stood in the middle with my hands outstretched, I could almost touch either side. It was hot, airless, and smelt awful. The galley only prepared food for the men working on the ship.

Eventually, I tired of exploring and went back out into the fresh sea air. I found a place to curl up, read my book, and eat some of the food in the wicker basket that Mummy had prepared for me. There were curd cheese sandwiches and my all-time favourite sandwich; grated chocolate on thickly buttered bread. There was a flask of tea, four small guavas, and three pieces of chocolate fudge. As the sun set, I went to see the skipper, who arranged a place for me to sleep in one of the cabins below deck.

By the time I woke up, we were already docking, right up to the harbour wall. I heard a lot of people running around, shouting orders. I gathered my belongings and headed for the stairs. Passengers were already filling the gangway. The line was so long that I feared I would never get off the boat.

Quietly and carefully, I crouched and slid between the grown-ups until I had reached the front of the line. Once there, I found that the skipper had already informed the customs officer about my passport. I was allowed to exit down the gangplank and into the crowded harbour office. I could hear Anne calling long before I could actually see anything other than her hat waving in the air.

"Coo-ee! Coo-ee, Janie over here." Her voice echoed loudly through the crowds.

I wondered what was in store for me this year. I loved coming to Trinidad; Anne was such a fun-loving, crazy person! I would be here for four long and incredible weeks.

She's Not Your Sister — She's Mine

Most of my memories of Anne were delightful. She was my surrogate mother, the impetus of my young life. She was my alter ego; I was quiet and painfully shy. She was loud, fearless, always calling out her famous 'Coo-ee' to people everywhere.

Mummy told me stories about Anne as a child in Australia. As a toddler, she once crawled under a horse and cart to play with the puppies. The driver freaked out, saying, "Oh lord, missus, please get your youngun' out from under there. That horse killed a man yesterday. Kicked 'em in the head."

As a nurse in London, she was the person who ran out into the street during an air raid to rescue some dog or child or elderly person and returned to the hospital unscathed. She was the one who had more names than the rest of the family put together and was never known by her birth name.

Anne never showed any embarrassment of her behaviour: driving through town with her hand on the horn, breaking the speed limit, and then patting the car, saying, "Slow down baby, slow down, you'll get me in trouble."

Once, driving on a wide double-lane road one day, Anne kept manoeuvring the car to hit the traffic cones in the median strip or central reservation. She hit the last one in the row and let out a whoop of joy, "OK, OK, little car, we'd better slow down now."

I was terrified that the police would stop her, might even take her away, even though she was White. But I was also exhilarated by her daring. The place we were going was a high-security prison in the Gulf of Paria, Carrera Island. I never understood why we took that trip, but Anne was unpredictable. We must have taken a ferry to the island, but all

I remember was being scared, staring at the barren ground of the island, and seeing big, angry-looking men staring at me.

If we kids fell over and hurt ourselves, all Anne ever said was, "Oops." She'd slap a dab of iodine on the cut and then say, "You are right as rain, now run off and play." Anne could smother you in hugs and kisses one moment and be shouting "hell and damnation" the next.

I loved staying with Anne and her family in the five-bungalow complex they owned. Anne and Gerry, her husband, whom I hardly ever saw, and their son, Bruce, lived in one unit. The other four units were rented. Their home was a three-floored house. The ground floor consisted of a large room divided into a living and dining space with a covered wooden causeway running along the outside. The causeway took a right-hand turn down a few steps and into a kitchen. It also turned left and became a flight of stairs to the first and second floors.

Bruce's bedroom was on the first floor. It was where Mummy and I usually stayed when we came to visit. One time, Gerry was away, and Mummy and I slept upstairs in the grand turret suite where Anne and Gerry usually slept. The room had dark wooden shutters on all four walls, which could be opened individually. I wanted to open all the shutters, leaving only the four corner posts holding up the roof.

Anne was not an organised or tidy person, except in this room. Here, Anne had beautiful embroidered white linens, dark wicker furniture, and rich brocade cushions scattered on the bed and chairs. Her lovely handmade clothes draped elegantly over the chairs and the vanity.

I loved it up there. I felt like a bird surveying the world. I could look straight down and see Mr. Chang, the Chinese man, on the veranda of the ground floor bungalow and the tops of all his animal cages. I could see the layout of Leanne's home at the bottom of the road. It was built around three sides of a large swimming pool. Bruce, when he was older, and I often went there in the afternoons with other children from the neighbourhood.

Mr. Chang had a variety of odd pets in cages, hanging on chains from the porch parapet. On Saturday mornings, we woke to a terrible "caterwauling," as Mummy called it, of animals in distress. I had never seen anyone bathe an animal before and was fascinated. But wet squirrels and blackbirds weren't a pretty sight, and soon I ran off to play elsewhere.

There was another bungalow behind Mr. Chang's, but I never saw the people who lived there. In the fourth bungalow, which was a separate building, lived a pretty lady who loved to bake cakes. She also had the only television in the area and the first I had ever watched; I was invited to visit in the early afternoons while Bruce took his nap. Once I overcame the surprise of seeing people running around in a square box, I loved the thrilling escapes and adventures and looked forward to my afternoon visits.

Outside the kitchen was a dirt trail that went into a bamboo forest. The stalks swayed and whistled in the wind. Hanging in the branches were dozens of tiny cone-shaped cocoon nests and the heady beating of hummingbirds' wings. While I stayed with Anne, I walked down the trail every day, crossed the ravine, and visited my best friend, Sarah Livingstone, who lived with her family on the other side; we looked like twins.

When I was younger, between eight and nine years old, Mummy came with me to Trinidad and we slept upstairs in Anne's room. One morning while we were their, Bruce announced, on getting out of bed, that he was going "up-tairs, go see Duggin," the name he called his grandmother. "See my sister."

Anne laughed, "She's my little sister, not yours."

"Nooo, she not your sister. She's mine," Bruce wailed.

His sobs brought Mummy and me hurrying downstairs to see what the matter was.

"I'll be your sister too, Brucy, don't cry," I said, wrapping my arm around him and giving him a big hug. Bruce sat on my lap, insisting on holding his favourite book, *The Little Engine that Could*, upside down and reading it word for word in his lispy baby voice; he knew the story so well.

Anne had a wonderful friend called Marn. She was often at their house with her son, John, Bruce's best friend. Marn was the softest, cuddliest person I had ever known. She had dark, laughing eyes, always smiling, with the kind of laugh that echoed through every fibre of her body and then radiated out to everyone else around her. I thought she was Swiss because she wore her long, thick hair, braided and wound around her head. The pictures I had seen of people with hair like hers were from Switzerland.

I turned ten the last time I visited Trinidad. Two events stand out in my memory. The first one, Anne was taking Bruce, the baby, Jeanne-

Marie, and me to Maracus Beach for the day. We had a wonderful time. I remember Bruce and me tumbling, laughing, into the back of the car when it was time to leave. Jeanne-Marie was asleep in the carrycot on the back seat. There were no car seats for babies, nor were there seatbelts for passengers in those days.

We had a long drive, at least an hour of mountainous switchbacks, before we would be home. Suddenly, there was a loud bang and breaking of glass, and Bruce and I were lying on the floor of the car on top of Jeanne-Marie, who was crying. She had been asleep in a carrycot behind the front seats. A car coming around the corner on the wrong side of the road hit us. No one was hurt but we had to wait for the police, which took a long time, and we couldn't stay in the car for some reason. I didn't want to see or talk to the police. I was embarrassed because I wasn't wearing any panties. I'd worn them as a bathing suit.

My other memory was perfection. Anne loved to sew, and every summer while I was in Trinidad, she made a couple of pretty dresses for me. That year, Anne made me my first grown-up dress. It was an olive green paisley, silky, shirt-waister with a gold, twisted cord belt. I flew home for the first time on the LIAT (Leeward Islands Air Transport). I wore my new dress under which I wore my first bra and white sandals. I felt like a movie star that day, walking down the gangway to the tarmac.

I did not run to meet Mummy, even though I was very excited to see her, but moved slowly, like a lady, with the rest of the passengers.

A Week With Daddy

We were sitting around the large dining room table eating dinner and for once, Daddy wasn't telling me to hurry up and finish my food. He wasn't covering his own food with pepper sauce, either. He was talking quietly to Mummy, which made me a little worried because it was unusual. I heard little pieces of the conversation. "Go to Mayreau..." "Give you a little peace and quiet."

"You can leave the table, Jane, if you are finished. Daddy and I still have things to talk about. Go wash up and get ready for bed."

I took a long time putting on my nightie, hoping to hear more of the conversation. They were talking about going somewhere. I was cleaning my teeth when I heard Daddy shout, "I need to talk to you, Janie, when you are done in the bathroom."

"I'm going to Mayreau, Janie, I have some work to do there. Would you like to come, take a holiday trip with me?"

"Oh yes, please, that sounds fun, Daddy. Is Mummy coming too?"

"No, Janie, she's going to stay here and take care of the chickens!" Daddy said, looking directly at Mummy, his face crinkled, with smiles, his pale blue eyes dancing with glee.

Mummy's answer was to flick the table napkin in his face. "Get away with yer. I'm going to enjoy the peace and quiet without the two of you under my feet all day."

"When are we leaving, Daddy?"

"Day after tomorrow. Early. Make sure you are ready to leave on time."

"You can pack your things in the morning; it's time for bed now." Then Mummy added, "Don't forget to say your prayers."

I said my prayers as always, asking Jesus to take pity on me and make me a better girl. Afterward, I always scoured the walls for cockroaches. I hated the scratching noises they made on the wall, I was paranoid of them falling on me. Both Mummy and Daddy thought it was foolishness, although Mummy was gentler about it.

Daddy and I left as the sun was rising. Mummy packed us a basket with hardboiled eggs, crackers and a flask of tea. Because we lived almost on the equator, our days began at six in the morning with the sunrise and ended when the sun disappeared twelve hours later.

Daddy and I bounced around in the old Citroën as he drove into Kingstown. He parked the car in a quiet spot at the harbour. We climbed aboard the tiny dingy belonging to the trawler we were travelling on; a man rowed us out to join the boat. I stood on the deck enjoying the wind and sea spray on my face as we motored out of the harbour, leaving Mummy at home alone with Bingo, Wong, the chickens, and the ducks.

I was going on a holiday with Daddy. It was something I had never done before. I had no idea why, but I was not about to ask. It wasn't important to know. I loved going on adventures, and this was going to be one.

"Do you want some breakfast, Janie? The galley cook is making scrambled eggs and bacon."

"I'll be down."

I took a look around the widening sea as we cruised out past the point. I looked back and saw the outline of Indian Bay, the Aquatic Club, and Fort Duvernette. I wondered what Mummy was doing at that moment, then turned and went down the stairs to have breakfast.

The trawler had a galley and a seating area right below the stairs, but the smell of diesel fuel and greasy food made me feel sick to my stomach. I tried to eat the eggs and bacon, but the bacon would not stay down. I hurriedly rushed up the stairs and ran to the stern to hang over the side.

I went back to the top of the stairs and called out, "Daddy, please, can I have your hankie, and can you bring me a few crackers from the basket Mummy packed for us. I can't come back down just yet."

The island of Bequia, Princess Margaret Island, was visible off the bow. Suddenly, there was a flash of silver and turmoil in the water. Sparkling like diamonds, a shoal of fish took off, flying through the air.

"Daddy, Daddy, come quickly. Come and see." As he emerged from the galley, I dragged him by the arm, "Look, look, isn't that beautiful? How do they do that?"

As another arc of silver and diamonds leapt from the water.

"They have a large pectoral fin that helps them leap out of the water."

"But why do they do that, Daddy?"

"To get away from the big fish that's chasing them. If you look over the edge, you might even see a sad swordfish who missed his lunch!"

I sighed, "Really?" I'd never read about a sad swordfish.

"Be careful, don't want you to become his lunch. We'd have to catch him and cut him open to rescue you."

"I'd be like Jonah." I had read all about Jonah and the whale in Auntie Gussie's *Encyclopedia Britannica*. I wondered if Daddy would be impressed with my knowledge.

"That's enough foolishness for now," Daddy said, bringing me back to earth. "Are you coming back down?"

"No thanks, Daddy, I'd rather stay up here," I said, giving him a surprised look — had he forgotten I was sick a little while ago? "It smells better up here, fresh and clean. I am going to pretend I am a princess on a tall ship sailing the rough seas in search of true love."

"You read too many books," he said with a smile. "I'm going below. Have fun."

"I will, Daddy."

By early afternoon, the boat pulled into the shallow waters of the island lagoon and anchored offshore. Daddy and I climbed down the ladder into the small dingy, and a Black man rowed us to the jetty with our food and belongings.

"I'd keep your hands in the boat, Janie. Look over the side."

Beneath the boat, and as far as I could see, were two-foot-long fishes with a long spike on their snouts.

"Are they barracuda?"

"No, they are probably swordfish or marlin."

"I won't be able to swim."

"They be garfish boss," the Black man said.

I looked up quickly at the Black man, willing him not to say anything else, then turned to Daddy, hoping to divert his attention. "What are garfish, Daddy? Will they hurt me?"

"They might do if you startle them. You will be able to swim, though. There is a beach on the other side of the island."

"See you in a week, eh boss?"

"Yes, pick us up on your way back to St. Vincent." Daddy gave a dismissive wave to the man as he rowed back to the boat.

We stood on the jetty surrounded by our belongings: my small yellow suitcase with brown straps, Daddy's battered brown one, a sack of potatoes and onions, and a box of tinned corned beef; our food for the week.

The family who lived on the island, a man and two small boys, met us with two donkeys. The father piled the suitcases and food onto one and asked if I wanted to ride the other. I wasn't sure at first because I was concerned it might throw me.

Daddy went ahead and boosted me up on the donkey. "It will be ok, Janie, go ahead and give it a try."

I didn't like looking down at the ground. It certainly seemed far away, but it was fun being higher than Daddy. Everything went well until we got to the top of the hill. Once over the top, the beast started going faster and faster.

"Daddy, stop him," I screamed. "He's going too fast!"

"Just hang on, Janie, you'll be ok. He's only going for the water, and it's not far to the ground."

The donkey did want to get a drink but when he reached the edge of the pond, he stopped quickly, I went right over his head and landed in the water. I wasn't hurt, just embarrassed at being wet and that Daddy and the island people laughed at me.

"Now, you don't need to go for a swim," Daddy said when the group reached the pond.

I glared at Daddy. Silly animal, I thought.

"Do you want to get back on?"

"Definitely not."

"It's uphill again from here."

"That's ok, I don't mind walking."

The tiny village located at the crest of the hill overlooked the Tobago Cays, Canouan, and Union Island. It was a breathtaking view; the green islands, set in a dazzling blue sea, with waves dancing in the sunlight, and delicate white coral shining through the clear water. The village consisted of two or three shanty houses, a small stone church, a schoolhouse, and two wooden cabins. We were staying in the smallest cabin.

"I'm going to explore, Daddy."

"Watch out for snakes!"

"I will," I said with a laugh. I knew this time Daddy was joking with me.

Still damp, I wandered off on my own for the few hours left before the sun dipped down into the sea with a brilliant flash of green. I continued over the top of the incline to the other side of the island to reach the lagoon.

It was beautiful; the sun on the sand smelt warm and salty. The waves ran into the cove like miniature, galloping horses riding softly over the fine white sand. I stopped and picked sea grapes along the shore. I sang and danced in the water, lay on my back on the wet sand, and watched the birds wheeling and dipping in the sky until the level of the sun told me it was time to return to the cabin, but I didn't want to leave. I loved the freedom of being myself. This is going to be a fun week, I thought.

"Good, glad you're back, Janie. I've been waiting for you. Are you ready to have dinner?"

"I'm so hungry I could eat a horse," I sang, skipping around the room.

"Go wash your hands. There is a pail outside the back door; use it sparingly."

Daddy lit the Tilley lamp and we had dinner in silence. I knew Daddy wasn't interested in my childish chatter. He'd made corned beef hash with the potatoes, onions, and the tinned corn beef we brought with us. Daddy said, "It's what I learnt to cook when I was in the army. It's a favorite of mine."

Mummy liked simple food with no spices, but I enjoyed food with lots of flavour. Daddy cooked everything in one pan over the kerosene stove. It was convenient and made clean-up very simple.

He would have cooked corned beef hash every night for dinner because that was all we had except for the goat's milk and the eggs for breakfast. We had leftover hash with that, too, until I decided to take a hand in our diet.

"Daddy?" I said after breakfast on the third day.

"Yes, Janie."

"Do you have a fishing hook or a bent pin?"

"Getting tired of my cooking, eh?"

"I thought it might be rather nice if I could catch some fish for you to fry up."

"Look in the toolbox under the house; you might find something."

I didn't find anything worth using, but I put on my swimsuit and sand shoes.

"I'm off, Daddy, I'll see you later. I'm going to be an explorer today and come home with plenty of treasure."

"Be good, have fun."

I decided to explore the old salt ponds first. The surface was dirty white and thickly cracked. I jumped and stamped on some edges, trying to break off a piece to taste. When I finally did, it tasted more like rusty iron than salt. I wasn't impressed.

"I'll collect some seawater in a jam jar and make my own salt; it'll taste better than this," I thought.

I found more sea grapes, riper this time, chased a few little creatures across the sands, and looked for red crabs. They were such fun to tease. The crabs loved to keep a tidy home and always threw out any foreign matter that went into their holes. It reminded me of when I first played this game.

The only other fruit was cacti. There wasn't enough fresh water on the island for much else to grow. I didn't know how to eat them without getting the spines stuck in my lips.

I tried fishing but not having a bent pin made it difficult to catch anything worth eating. The little fish were too hard to grab with my hands. They kept slipping through my fingers.

I tied my sand shoes together and hung them around my neck so that they didn't get wet as I climbed around the rocks on the far side of the cove to the harbour lagoon. I kept my eyes peeled for those garfish. I found some large shellfish clinging to the rocks. I knew what they were because I had asked Daddy about the broken shiny shells I had collected the day before.

"These will make a great dinner. Daddy said he likes to eat mussels, and they just go into boiling water," I thought.

I looked for the biggest ones, pulling them off the rocks with my hands. I filled my bucket with the mussels. My fingers got a workout that day. Daddy and I had a wonderful dinner that night. Afterward, I read my storybook by the light of the Tilley lamp, *Five go to Billycock Hill*, before going to bed. Enid Blyton's stories were some of my favourite books.

All that week, I rose with the sun and rolled out of the army camp cot. If I wasn't careful, the cot tipped me out with a thump on the floor.

Daddy had the bedroom with a metal-framed bed and a thick horsehair mattress. I dressed quickly, splashed a scant cup of water over my face, then went to look for Daddy.

I usually found him sitting in a cane chair on the verandah, smoking, wearing only his cotton vest and khaki shorts. After breakfast, I was free to wander anywhere on the island. I'd come back to the cabin when the sun was high in the sky and have lunch with Daddy. I had to rest on the camp bed for an hour or two, and then I'd be off again until the sun went down. On one of the days, I saw a couple of the boys eating cacti.

"How do you do that?" I asked after watching them for a while.

"It be easy, you wan' me show' yer?"

"Does it taste good?"

"Oh, yer man, swee' as hon'y."

"You promise, you aren't trying to fool me? I'll tell my dad if you try to trick me."

"Why you tink we try to trick yer? Look this 'ere 'ow to eat witout gettin' dem pricks in da mout," he said. "Now you do try it."

I did as the boy demonstrated and was pleased to see they were impressed with how well I slit and folded back the skin and sucked out the juices. I was relieved that it did not burn my mouth like the bird peppers when I had started school in St. Vincent, but I wasn't very impressed with the flavour.

All too soon, it was time to leave the island of Mayreau and go home. I was excited to see Mummy again and find out how she had managed without us. I was especially excited to see Bingo. I expected he'd be happy to see me, wagging his tail like crazy and running around in circles. I'd promised him I'd take him for a long walk in the hills and tell him all about my adventures when I came back home.

On the homeward journey, the only excitement was watching a pod of porpoises, racing and leaping off the bow of the trawler. I stayed on deck this time and didn't feel sick. I loved watching the passing islands and watching the coast of St. Vincent growing closer and closer.

"Let's pick up dinner at the market before we head for home, Janie."

"Don't stop and talk, will you, Daddy. I want to get home quickly."
I knew he sometimes stopped to buy a bottle of rum, and I wanted Mummy to be happy to see us.

"Ok, ok, Janie, I'll be quick," Daddy said with a laugh. "It will be nice to be home again. I love my Edie so much. I just don't know how to tell her that."

On the way home, Daddy even joined in when I started singing. We sang "Olde King Cole was a Merry Olde Soul" and a few other songs. It was a happy drive home to Mummy.

One Sunny Day

It was the summer of 1960. Mummy, Daddy and I, stood watching from the large terminal windows of the Arnos Vale Airport for the LIAT (Leeward Island Air Transport) to taxi to a halt. I was excited to see my cousin Bruce and sister Anne. It had been a year since I had seen them, and Anne was bringing her nine-month baby, Jeanne-Marie, for the first time. The three of them were coming from Trinidad to stay for two weeks.

"Look, Mummy! There, they're coming now."

Anne was coming down the gangway, her full skirt billowing in the wind. The air hostess was behind her, carrying the baby and holding Bruce's hand. It was a lovely sight.

"Coo-ee!" Anne's voice rang out across the tarmac.

Mummy had tears in her eyes as we walked towards the small group. She was eager to see and hold her latest grandbaby.

Jeanne-Marie was a delightfully cheery baby who cooed like a "lovebird" Mummy said, when she was picked up and cuddled. She had a peaches-and-cream complexion, and when she smiled, her blue-green eyes sparkled like diamonds.

Bruce was thrilled to have his very own baby sister, and I didn't mind not being his sister anymore. Anne was relaxed and happy. The family she'd wanted for so long was finally complete. She had been so sad when she'd lost her first child three years before Bruce was born. I remember hearing that he was a blue baby. Anne named that baby Maximillian.

Daddy drove us back to the house in Calliaqua for a lunch of chicken sandwiches, followed by Mummy's special chocolate cake. I was eager to take Bruce to see the new wattled house I had built.

"Can Bruce and I leave the table, please, Mummy?"

"It's OK, off you go. I'll call you when it's time to come in again."

"Come on Bruce, let's go. I've made a special house for us to play in. Stand still a minute, Bruce, I have something for you," I said after we had left the house. I took two small green badges out of my pocket, and pinned one onto my dress and one onto Bruce's shirt.

"There you are. Now you are an honorary member of the secret Busy Bees Club."

"Why bithy bees?" Bruce lisped.

"I don't know, just because."

"Why because?"

"Oh no, not that still. Please Bruce, come on, let go. I want to play."

"Okey dokey," Bruce replied.

I giggled. He sounded so funny when he said that, just like his mum. The badges were made from two oblong pieces of cardboard. I covered them with green silk and carefully hemmed all around the edges. On the front, I embroidered two large B's in red stem stitch. On the back, I over-sewed a safety pin on each badge. We walked around the wattled house a few times and stared out of the window. There was nothing else to do, so we left and went down to the river.

"Maybe you can help me make some furniture for the house, Bruce?"

"Oh yes, please, let's."

"Let's go to the river now and bring back some wood. Then we can ask Daddy, oh, Grandpa to you, for hammer and nails, and we can start tomorrow. We can all have a picnic here tomorrow."

We would not make any furniture the next day or ever have a picnic in the wattled house.

We went swimming at the Aquatic Club the next day instead. I was happy that I had finally learnt to swim and loved to jump off the jetty and swim back to shore. I always jumped off the first platform to the side and never off the very end of the jetty where it was too deep for me to stand; I was still afraid of deep water.

Bruce, a chubby happy, three-year-old, loved to stand on the step shouting, "Tatch me, Jane, tatch me," and launch himself off into the air. I would catch him as he hit the water. We'd both go under together and come up spluttering and laughing. "Aga'n, aga'n."

It was delightful having Bruce here to play with. It made swimming much more fun. There was a French family there that day with a little girl about two years of age. I saw her watching Bruce jump in a couple of times, then she launched herself at me without warning. Fortunately, she was very close and I grabbed her. I watched for her coming along the jetty from that moment on, afraid that I might not see her and she'd drown.

My fears were unfounded, and I had a lot of fun playing with Bruce and the little girl.

Each time I jumped into the water, I looked toward the beach and saw Mummy sitting on a chair with her large straw hat shading her face. She was always sewing or reading. From time to time, she would see me and wave. Daddy was inside at the bar talking shop with the other men whose wives and children were outside swimming. At one point, he brought Bruce and me a Coke, which was a wonderful treat. Anne was in the water, holding Jeanne-Marie on her chest, and then she sat on the beach with Mummy while the baby slept. It was a wonderfully happy day.

It was almost dusk by the time we were ready to leave. I remember thinking Jeanne-Marie was overdressed for such a warm evening. She had on yellow dungarees with teddy bears and spinning tops on them, and her pretty plump cheeks were flushed pink. Underneath her dungarees, she wore a cotton vest, a long-sleeved shirt, plus a towelling nappy and plastic pants to keep her clothes dry.

Once home, Anne laid the baby down in the cot, still fully clothed.

"Can I put on her nightie?" I asked.

"Don't fuss, Janie; she's OK. Let sleeping dogs lie. I'll do it later."

When I woke up the next day, Anne had gone out, leaving Jeanne-Marie still asleep, fully clothed. Mummy seemed worried, checking on the baby every few minutes.

Suddenly she was shouting. "Clem! Clem, come quickly. I need the tin tub filled with ice water now."

I heard Daddy say, "Oh my God," and rush into the kitchen.

Daddy moved very fast whenever there was an emergency. He had grabbed the tin bathtub from under the table, the ice pick from the shelf, and smashed the block of ice before I had a chance to ask what was wrong.

I followed Daddy into the bedroom to see what was happening but stopped in the doorway, horror-struck. Mummy had stripped Jeanne-Marie of all her clothes. Her little body was the colour of a dark purple overripe Java plum, jerking and shaking, with white spittle coming out of her mouth.

"Jane! Go now, see if you can find Anne and tell her to come home at once."

I was out the door running, never thinking that I had no idea where

Anne might be or how long it would take me to find her. I do not remember whether I even brought Anne home.

The next thing I remember, we were all at the hospital. Jeanne-Marie lay unconscious, looking small and shrivelled in the large bed. She wasn't blue anymore, but very pale.

"What's wrong, Mummy?" Bruce asked, trying to climb up onto Anne's lap as she sat on the bed.

"Your sister's very sick," Anne said. "You've got to be a good boy and not bother Mummy at the moment."

"Tuddle me, Mummy," Bruce whined, but Anne ignored him, too worried to give him any notice.

"Come to Granny sonny, come upsy,"

Bruce continued to cry and hang onto Anne until Mummy finally picked him up.

"Come on, Jane, let's take Bruce out into the garden."

Jeanne-Marie remained in Kingstown General Hospital for seven days with Anne constantly by her side before she recovered consciousness. Then, they all flew back to Trinidad.

Not long afterward, they moved as a family to a remote location on the island of Tortola in the British Virgin Islands. I did not see them again for over six years. Those years separated us all.

Mummy and Daddy were unhappy with Anne going to a place without good medical care. I missed Bruce and going to Trinidad in the summer. Subconsciously, I blamed Anne for leaving too many clothes on Jeanne-Marie when she put her to bed.

—❖·◉·❖—

Jeanne-Marie never fully recovered from her vaccine encephalitis. I overheard talk about a new vaccine, the Salk vaccine for polio. Also, I heard Mummy telling Daddy that she was against Anne taking the baby for her inoculations at the clinic in San Fernando, Trinidad.

Jeanne-Marie's brain damage left her with right-sided hemiplegia. It caused her to lurch sideways when walking, to have slurred speech, and to have grand-mal seizures for the rest of her life.

When I saw the family again after their time in Tortola, my heart broke for the beautiful baby I remembered when I was a child of eleven years. Jeanne-Marie behaved like a wild animal, and Bruce was a traumatised young boy. But when she sang, which was often, she had the voice of an angel, especially when she sang "Jesus Wants Me for a Sunbeam."

Jeanne-Marie died in an adult family home in Canada at thirty years of age. The cause was listed as accidental drowning.

More Christmas Surprises

Once we moved to Calliaqua, life became more settled, but even I knew there was little money to spare. The traditional pine and fir trees for Christmas were expensive because they came from North America and Canada. After our first year at Sunningdale, Daddy created alternative trees.

"We can't afford a Christmas tree this year, Janie," he said.

"Christmas won't be the same without a tree, Daddy," I said sadly.

"It will still be special, you'll see. We'll have a white Christmas this year."

"A white Christmas? What do you mean, Daddy?"

"You'll see."

Daddy used white-wash or distemper to spray-paint the old fir tree from the previous year. It had been left behind the old outhouse since last year. Until I saw it, I couldn't imagine how Daddy could make a dead tree look good. It was beautiful. It looked like the trees on the cards we received from England, all covered in snow and glistening under the lighted candles and sparkling tinsel and coloured glass balls.

"Just like being back in the old country," Mummy said with tears in her eyes.

Another year, we had a young cherry tree. Its delicate small green leaves sparkled with Christmas joy. I had my own mini artificial tree, which I decorated for my dolls. I now had ten large dolls, which I played with all the time.

Each year, Mummy made and wrapped two dresses for each of my dolls. I made small books from lined paper cut from school books, adding brown paper covers which I stitched along one edge. I made a couple of satchels from soft leather as my gifts for the larger dolls. A couple months before the Christmas of my eleventh year, a couple of my smaller dolls disappeared. I searched everywhere.

"Do you know where they are, Mummy?" I asked.

"Maybe you just left them outside."

I knew better than to argue with her when she said that, but I knew that wasn't true. I took great care of my dolls. I treated them as if they were my children. I was upset but tried to put them out of my mind.

This was the Christmas Daddy built me a dollhouse. It was a bungalow with three rooms and a verandah that ran the width of the rooms. The roof also opened so I could get inside from the top. Mummy and Daddy had furnished the bungalow with a sofa and chairs made from wood, cardboard, and fabric. There was a wooden bed with a straw mattress and tiny sheets. Also, two bedside tables in the bedroom. Daddy built a larger table for the kitchen and a small stove with a metal ring on top.

Mummy hung curtains in the windows and made clothes for a family of dolls, which included my two missing dolls. Mummy dressed them as grownups, the parents of the doll-children of the house. Mummy made a jacket and trousers for the male doll, coloured the hair, and added a beard and moustache. The female doll wore a blue dress with a belt around her waist and grey and brown hair from strands of wool. There was also a baby doll in a diaper, in a crib. I was ecstatic and furious.

"You did take them, Mummy, I knew you did, but I love them! Thank you so much," I cried, hugging them both. I played with my dollhouse until I left the island. Mummy and Daddy gave it to the children's ward of the hospital where Jeanne-Marie had been.

The following year was different. Mummy had an accident a few days before Christmas. She rarely wore shoes in the house, and she stepped onto a T-bone Bingo had been chewing in the living room. The bone punctured the bottom of her foot. She couldn't walk on it for the whole holiday because it was too painful.

"I'm sorry, Jane, you will have to help me decorate the tree this year. I won't be able to do it on my own, and Daddy seems the worse for wear."

He did seem to be more morose and often went to the village and came home drunk. Still, it was fun to unwrap the decorations and hang them on the tree, along with all the strands of tinsel. But it wasn't the same as waking up to the surprise of a decorated tree and presents underneath. That year, I realised that the real magic of Christmas was Mummy. She put a great deal of work into the twelve days of Christmas to make them particularly special for me. She always followed the twelve days of Christmas rule. The tree went up on Christmas Eve and came down on the sixth of January. Everything was then carefully wrapped and packed away that day until the following year.

Helping to decorate the tree helped me to overcome my greatest disappointment. I knew some presents came from England and searched until I found them. I opened one carefully. It was an exquisite gold-coloured metal purse brooch. I was thrilled; I couldn't wait until Christmas to open the rest. But sadly, I didn't wait. I kept sneaking a peek into the presents until there were no surprises left for Christmas Day.

Daddy also came home late for dinner and drunk. He tripped over my mini tree, breaking the glass balls. Mummy was tired because she had struggled to cook because of her foot injury. I saw her glare at Daddy, her face white and tight-lipped. I don't think she realised I was watching, but when their eyes met, she ran her finger across her throat. I knew that meant, "I'd rather slit your throat than look at you." I heard her say it before, usually sarcastically. This time she seemed to mean it! I was tense, nervous, and panic-stricken. Daddy went to give me a hug, but I pushed him away, burst into tears, grabbed my mini tree, and threw it through the door onto my bed.

"This is the worst Christmas ever," I shouted. "You have ruined everything. I hate you." I stayed in my room for a long time before coming out and putting my arms around Mummy. I knew I had also ruined Christmas. "I'm sorry, Mummy, can we have still have dinner all together?"

"Go see if your father's sobered up and tell him to come to the table. I'm sure the chicken and the vegetables are still warm."

"The pudding will be delicious." I interrupted.

"Off you go. Then come back and help me with putting the dishes on the table."

I was glad Mummy never believed in letting the sun go down on your anger.

A Dangerous Adventure

When I finished reading *The Kon-Tiki Expedition*, written by Thor Heyerdahl, I was excited to build my own raft. I knew that a cork tree was growing at the end of our land, down by the river.

One morning, I borrowed Daddy's axe, climbed the tree, and started cutting a limb. It was much harder than I had imagined. The axe bounced back at me every time I hit the wood. I soon realised that making a raft was not going to be easy. I struggled for a while but gave up after only cutting one branch. I thought I might hit myself with the axe if I wasn't careful and that I had better not continue.

I still wanted to go to Youngs Island, a short distance across the channel from the Aquatic Club, at Villa. I had enjoyed going with Daddy in a glass-bottomed boat around Youngs Island and Rock Fort. The coloured fish and the coral were exquisite, magnified through the glass. But I wanted to have my own adventure. Building a raft was my original solution. Now I had to think of a different way to get there.

As no adult would lend me their boat without Daddy being there too, I decided that the only way I could get there was to swim. The clubhouse wasn't open during the daytime, and once I had made my decision to swim across the span of deep water to Youngs Island, I foolishly didn't tell anyone. It was my adventure, and I thought it would be an excellent way to improve my swimming. Youngs Island was uninhabited when I lived in St. Vincent and was usually only visited by boat. I didn't have to worry about being run down by the Grumman Goose seaplane because this was a weekday, and the plane only operated on weekends when it took tourists to one of the other small islands.

It took me the best part of an hour to swim to the island, floating when I became tired. There were moments when I remembered that the channel was very deep, unfathomable, I had heard. Also, barracudas were believed to live in these waters. When my fantasies ran riot and I thought of being attacked by those vicious fish, I would turn over onto my back and float for a while, kicking quietly not to make too much of a splash. "I can do this," I told myself.

When I finally reached the shore, I lay on the sparkling sand, which looked like millions of tiny diamonds glistening in the sunshine, and soaked up the warmth for a while before deciding to explore. It was easier to walk around the island than go over the top because there were so many bushes and rocks, and it was hard to clamber through. My roaming took me around the island to the Atlantic side and Fort Duvernette, a 190-foot volcanic rock looming out of the water. At the top were two cannons erected by the British to protect the fort from invaders in the 1800s. There were 225 steps carved into the face of the fort to get to the top.

The distance between Youngs Island and Fort Duvernette didn't seem very far, maybe fifty feet, no further than the length of our house. I knew I could do it if I was careful. The clear water swirled, swelled, and eddied from both sides of the fort, meeting in the middle with an uprush curl of water. During the eddy, it was a little over ankle deep. I decided to go for it, paying close attention to the black sea urchins and where I placed my feet. I was not sure if they were poisonous, but I did know that if I put my foot down on one of them, the spines would break off in my feet and be very painful to remove. I had seen it happen to Daddy. I had watched him from the doorway of his bedroom as he soaked his foot in a strong, hot mustard bath, a traditional English remedy for, among other things, opening up the pores and helping to rid the skin of the toxic spines. Daddy cursed and swore. "Damn and blast, damn and blast."

This was just my kind of adventure. I liked being alone with a challenge. It was the only way to go. I crouched-walked so I could lift my feet off the sea-bed when the water rushed around the rock. Then, I carefully placed my feet down when the water was clear, avoiding those nasty, spiky creatures until I reached the fort. Some sea urchins are a delicacy, but I never ate them as they were usually served raw, and I never wanted to eat a live creature.

I climbed those stairs and viewed the world from the top. I imagined I was a soldier on cannon duty but knew that I could not fire on any ship. On the way down those hundreds of steps, I imagined that I was on a deserted island and there were pirates after me. The only way to escape was to go around the island again and swim back to the mainland as fast as possible.

By the time I returned to the other side of Youngs Island, it was already getting late. I had expended a lot of energy. I was already tired and apprehensive of the swim back to Villa. It took much longer than an hour to swim. I floated on my back much of the time, kicking my feet to propel myself along. By the time I reached the Aquatic Club, the sun was going down, and I was cold and exhausted. I was able to have a warmish shower in the clubhouse cubicle, change into my shorts and shirt before getting back on my bike and cycling the mile or so home.

In answer to the question as to where I had been, I replied that I had swum to Youngs Island. Mummy's only reply was to say, "Thank goodness you learnt to swim first, and the barracudas weren't hungry."

I fell into a deep and dreamless sleep that night, totally worn out but very happy to be tucked up in my bed and no nightmares about being eaten by the barracuda!

Black Magic and Witchcraft

It was one of those beautifully warm nights with a slight breeze. Stepping out of the bathroom, I stopped a moment at the open door, watching the fireflies light up the dark sky. At that moment, I heard an eerie sound floating through the air.

"Hel-up! Hel-up. The devil done throw me d-d-down," a voice quavered.

"Mummy, Mummy," I shouted as I ran into the dining room. "I think someone is hurt. I think they are out in the field."

Mummy put down the sewing she was working on and went to the back door. I stood back a little way. The voice floated out of the darkness again.

"Hell-p me, hell-p me. I done lo-ost meself in this h-here p-place."

Mummy laughed softly, "Go, get me the torch from Daddy's bedside table."

Daddy looked up as I ran into his bedroom. "What are you after, Janie."

"Just getting the torch for Mummy."

"What's she up to, Janie?"

"Don't know, but it sounds like someone is in the field and can't find their way out."

"Bet it's that damn darkie, drunk as a coot again."

Mummy took the torch and stepped outside. "You stay by the door, Jane. I'll see if I can guide Ryan back to the house and get him back on the road home."

Ryan lived with his woman in the shack on the small field bordering ours. His black skin was like old worn leather and the whites of his eyes were often bloodshot, reminding me of the carnival demon. It made me a little afraid of him when he had his bouts with the "demon" rum. Otherwise, he was a quiet man.

125

"Ryan, is that you out there?"

"Oh Mam, tis me. The devil done turn me around and throw me down."

"Can you see the torchlight, Ryan? If you can follow the beam, I'll get you out of there."

It took a while, but eventually, Mummy guided Ryan out of the field to the back door.

He couldn't stop thanking her. "Thank ye, Mam, thank ye, Mam. You done save me from the devil!"

"Don't be a damn fool, man. You're drunk. Sit down on the step and I'll clean up the cut on your head."

Mummy sent me to get a clean cloth and antiseptic from the bathroom and then told me to get ready for bed. The blood dripping from his head was a deep red. It made me think of the two men in Back Street. Ryan seemed so sure that it had been the devil who threw him into the ditch that I was scared enough to believe him, despite Mummy's matter-of-fact reply.

I was still sure the devil existed: I was convinced that I had seen his face in Montserrat when I was seven. I heard people, Black and White, talking in whispers about those who practised witchcraft in the mountains and the devil they conjured up. The drums beat when the moon was high and on nights when it was so dark that even the stars didn't seem to shine. The rhythm of those drums echoed down the valley to where we lived. They vibrated in my head, and a nauseous wave of fear would run through me until I had to drown out the sound by putting my head under the pillow. I was afraid the drums might conjure up the devil and steal my spirit.

One night, the drums were loud. I felt that they beat in anger, and the dark cloudless sky seemed filled with sadness. They continued to reverberate long into the night and deep into my dreams. They seemed to say, "Run run, we're going to get yer."

Ma Vernon, as we called her, was an Obeah woman. She lived in the inner region of the Mesopotamia Mountains. To Mummy, she was just an old woman, caught up in the past. Ma Vernon wore a white cloth wrapped around her head and over her ears with sticks stuck into it. She was a sorceress or witch to those who feared her.

One night, I dreamed of Ma Vernon sitting outside a wooden shack surrounded by trees. She sat on a low stool in front of an open fire, chanting words I could not understand and stirring herbs into a pot. Sparks flew up around Ma Vernon, and I saw a group of men standing behind her, each holding large rocks in their hands, ready to stone her. I wanted to scream out, "Ma Vernon, look behind you!" She continued chanting until the stones fell.

A few days later, I saw Mummy sitting at the dining room table after breakfast with her head in her hands, the newspaper spread out in front of her.

"What's wrong, Mummy?"

"Ma Vernon's dead."

"Oh!" I felt faint. I'd dreamt, again, of a terrible thing before it happened. This time, it was much worse.

"What happened, Mummy. How did she die?"

"She was found dead yesterday morning by the mountain police."

"She was old though, wasn't she, Mummy?" I said hopefully.

"Not really dear, but she didn't die of old age, unfortunately. The police believe that she was murdered."

I said nothing, afraid Mummy might look up and see my stricken face. I had not told Mummy about the previous dream I had about the man on Sion Hill, stealing the pretty dress I made for Jeanne-Marie.

"The world's a strange place, Jane, and the people in it even stranger. Just run along outside, dear, and see what Daddy's doing. Leave me alone for a while."

I was glad to get away, but I didn't go to Daddy. I climbed up in the avocado tree and cried. I thought of Ma Vernnon as a simple, kind, old woman with pencils sticking out of her head.

I remembered how Ma Vernon would stop and give Mummy some small packages of herbs in exchange for coins we collected from our ice sales. She sometimes had a piece of fruit for me, a ripe shiny plumrose, a couple of yellow hog plums, or akees. She usually asked me to pick her a flower from the garden in exchange.

Soonie, the Black girl who lived across our road, was probably five or more years older than me. She did our washing and ironing once or twice a week. At first, she was nice and friendly, even letting me iron the handkerchiefs and table napkins or making me cassava milk with golden syrup. Later, whenever she had the chance, she'd pick on my fears. At first, beating her fingers against the ironing board and humming. Both actions made me nervous.

Then, with a knowing laugh, she'd say, "Ye'd better spread salt over ye mattress 'fore makin' the bed." And that I should be careful leaving the room. "You'd wanna a'ways be a-like me. I a'ways walk out dem door backwards on me bare feet. Dem zombies not get yer den."

"You really do that, Soonie? Every morning?"

She'd laugh, kind of shrill but low, so Mummy wouldn't wonder what was going on.

One day, Bingo and I crept quietly up the path alongside Soonie's hut, hoping she wouldn't see me. I was going to the woods above, but she came out and grabbed me by the arm.

"I got to teach yer whitie, a few dem facts o'life."

I struggled, wanting to scream, but didn't, afraid Mummy or Daddy would hear me. I wasn't supposed to take this shortcut to the road above.

"I'd got yer. No bother tryin' to struggle." Soonie dragged me inside the hut. "Yer jest sit there and keep that dog quiet. Don't go leavin' until I tell yer."

When I sat down on the box seat, I noticed a rooster tied by the foot and a rag around its eyes. I thought she might be planning to kill it in front of me. Bingo laid down with his nose on the ground, growling softly in his throat. Soonie's voice grew louder and more gravelly, as though the sound was coming from the bottom of her feet. I felt forced to keep my eyes on Soonie. I watched her pick up a dirty paper bag containing a bottle.

"In this bottle, I fix de rum with guinea peppers, garlic. I drink it to ward off all evil."

She tipped her head back and drank and began gyrating, slowly at first, then faster, her hips swinging closer and closer to my face. Her thick red lips glistened with a mixture of lipstick and perspiration. I raised my hands to hide my face.

"Please let me go home."

Tossing back her head, she laughed a shrill cackle. "White bitch, take dem hand from doses eyes, look, see what men done want. If dey don't get it, dey does rip yer heart out."

I put my fingers in my ears and closed my eyes, and leaned against Bingo's fur. He was now sitting on his haunches, a louder growl in his throat. As Soonie moved faster and faster, she started removing her clothes, her interest in me gone.

"Now, Bingo, come," I whispered. I slid out of the door and ran home with Bingo beside me.

I never breathed a word to anyone, but I no longer wanted to iron the handkerchiefs or be anywhere near Soonie. I found reasons to leave the house when she was coming.

You're a Good Girl

As I became older, I didn't ask many questions of anyone. I was a good girl. I was about twelve when I remember coming home and whispering to Mummy, "I need to ask you something." I insisted that we hide in the wardrobe in the bedroom, but she refused, so I pulled one of her dresses out and folded it around me, whispering, "What does F***ing H*** mean?"

In her usual pragmatic way, Mummy replied, "It is not a nice word, and good girls never say it, so you won't again, will you?"

"No, Mummy," I replied, letting go of the dress and running outside. "Bingo, Bingo, let's go."

I remember Mummy had two phrases she often used, especially if I began asking questions. One was the proverb, "Curiosity killed the cat," and the other was a line or two from a poem by Tennyson. "Mine is not to reason why, mine is just to do or die." Neither made much sense to me at the time. But I did understand there was an implication that being too curious might be dangerous. I also wasn't supposed to reason "why," just accept.

Back when I was just over seven and fell through the rafters of my friend's barn, Mummy didn't question or reprimand me as to why I was up there in the first place. I stayed home and did the things I loved doing, reading, puzzles and helping Mummy with her patchwork. Even when I had the terrible accident, being a "bad fairy" in Calliaqua, there were no questions. I was just swooped up and taken to the doctor. Mummy never insisted on being with me. I had to 'do or die,' as the poem said.

Mummy never explained the facts of life; why as a girl, I was different from boys, or what might happen when I was older. The only males in my life, except Daddy, were Douglas and my cousins, whom we hadn't seen since we left Barbados, and the two younger neighbour boys, Graham and Thomas, in Monserrat, and Noel, in St. Vincent.

Anne explained about monthly bleedings and bought me my first bra the last year I was in Trinidad. But there was confusion about babies. Anne's explanation left me believing that a baby would grow inside me whether I wanted it to or not when I was twenty-one!

After the tragedy of Jeanne-Marie, it was as if the whole world broke apart, little by little. Nothing felt the same anymore. Mummy seemed sad, more wrapped up in her own space. I often saw tears in her eyes, but she would brush me aside if I tried to cuddle her or ask questions. Daddy drank more and more, and my nightmares became more frequent and terrifying.

It was a comfort when Daddy drew me onto his lap at night and cuddled me when I went to kiss him goodnight. My innocent naivety made me indifferent to Daddy running his hands under my nightdress and between my legs. "You're a good girl," he'd say. "Now run along and say goodnight to your mother." I just wanted to be cuddled and held. I would kiss him happily and run off to bed, hoping not to dream.

I was about twelve and a half years of age when I met Margie. We were both cycling up the long, curving Dorcester Hill Road. She lived about the halfway mark to my house. She invited me to stop off at her home and play for a while before I continued on my way. Margie went to a different school, but she had lots of books, and I loved reading. Her mother worked, but her father was at home. After a while, we stopped playing together, and only her father was in the house when I stopped by. He told me I could continue to come by any time and read.

At first, I knew he was around the house, but I did not see him. Then, occasionally he'd come into my friend's bedroom, where I was reading, and ask if I would like a drink or a biscuit. After a while, he'd come and sit on the bed, and ask me what I was reading. I thought he was being kind and friendly. I didn't consider him a stranger, he was Margie's dad, and I didn't understand that it wasn't wise to be alone with a man. I was fortunate he never got beyond touching me between the legs before I stopped going to Margie's house.

After I left St. Vincent, I heard he went to prison, convicted of abuse and rape.

Soonie's menacing behaviour after grabbing me while taking the shortcut past her hut had really scared me. I was determined to be a good girl and only do what I was told from then on.

I never knew whether Mummy guessed about Daddy, Margie's father, Soonie, or any of my traumas. I only realised in writing my story, how her choice of not talking openly about the facts of life with me impacted my own behaviour. I knew nothing about my body, how it developed, and why males might be interested in me. It is possibly why I was never told about going to England. To paraphrase Mummy, "Mine was not to reason why...just to do or die."

We can't always prevent what is done to us, but we can hope to survive it.

The Last Hurricane

The silence lay like a heavy blanket in the hot, sultry, stillness of the afternoon. My starched white calico blouse clung to my back, damp and limp. I pushed my hand through my lank hair and sighed, lifted the lid of my desk, and took a quick peek at the scripture book laid open inside. It was so hard remembering a whole chapter of the gospels, including paragraphs, commas, and full stops. The previous night, I spent hours revising.

The clanging school bell brought my desk lid to a quick close: my heart thumped hard. Mother Superior entered the room and stood at the front of the class.

"Children, sit up straight. I have an announcement," she said in her quiet, authoritative voice. "Please pack up quietly and go home immediately. There is a hurricane warning in process."

I remember being amazed that in times of crisis, no one stopped for prayer. We obeyed the *holy order* and filed out of the room. It was the 26th of September, 1963. The strongest and deadliest hurricane in history, Hurricane Flora, was about to hit St. Vincent.

I, fortunately, had long since outgrown my terror of such warnings. I had buried my insecurities, but my knees still shook as I mounted my bicycle and cycled out of town. I had been through two major hurricanes before: Hurricane Janet, while we lived in Barbados, and Hurricane Audrey, in Montserrat. Calliaqua, on a normal day, was an hour away. Now I would race to get home quicker.

I had five miles to cycle home, at least two of them uphill if I took the long, slow, but safe and easy hill that wound itself up and around the outlying houses of the town. Or, I could go straight up the other side, though the poor part of town, which made me afraid, but it would cut a few miles off my journey. I chose the shortcut through Sion Hill.

I cycled fast along the gentle hill into town, past Mr. Manion, the shopkeeper, on the corner. He was too busy to wave. Along Middle Street, where the ringing of hammers rose and fell as the shopkeepers battened down their windows with large pieces of wood kept especially for these occasions. I sweated up the steep side of the hill, dismounting and running with my bike when I could no longer pedal hard enough. I was thirteen now, and Mummy and Daddy needed my help.

Flying down Dorsetshire Hill Road, I cycled past the entrance to Auntie Gussie's house and the sharp bend where the old driveway of Arnos Vale met the road. It was a beautiful day, not a cloud in sight. There was no wind in the trees, no birds singing, but the air was still and muggy. I pushed myself to ride hard. Down across the flat land of the airstrip and up past Indian Bay and the Aquatic Club. I took another shortcut across the top of the hill before the drop down into Calliaqua. I turned right at the Java plum tree and the asylum, down the foot trail, across the river, and home.

Once home, I changed my clothes quickly. Daddy sent me up on the galvanised roof to hammer in all the loose nails; the nails came loose with the heat of the sun and the cool of the evenings. It was too dangerous for Daddy to climb onto the roof. We had no shutters on this house, so Daddy nailed boards diagonally across the windows for protection. Wong and Bingo were inside, and we brought the chicken coop into the kitchen.

Inside, I helped Mummy hang blankets over the windows to protect against flying glass, just in case the boards were ripped away. Pictures and mirrors were placed on the floor under the beds. We put the crystal bowl into the cedar chest. It was very precious to Mummy because it had travelled with her from England to Australia, and then to the Caribbean.

We dragged the dining room table against the wall; our additional protection in case of a building collapse. We ate dinner sitting on the floor, our backs against the table with Wong purring in Mummy's lap, and Bingo lying between Daddy and me.

That night, we played cards by the warm glow of a Tilley lamp and listened to the wind as it whipped along the edge of the roof, the rain pounding like hands beating on steel drums until it was time to sleep. We slept curled together underneath the upended table. I fell asleep to Mummy counting slowly between the cracks of lightning, which lit the room through the blankets, and the claps of thunder. Each second counted, equalled one mile from the storm.

I woke to the whine and fuzz of Daddy tuning the wireless. "The worst is over. The wind is finally changing, moving south." Daddy declared.

The hurricane passed with little or no damage to our home. Later, we heard on the radio that Hurricane Flora had landed on Tobago, the wind ripping galvanised roofs from homes, and driving them through trees. The damage was so devastating that it changed the island economy forever, from cash-crop agriculture to tourism and fishing. Hurricane Flora travelled on to leave over seven thousand dead in Haiti and Cuba before burning out.

Daddy got up in the morning to check on the damage outside. Our stony road was now a rushing six-foot-wide river! We worked together to return the house to normal, then I went to play in the river. The water, the colour of milky tea, rushed around my legs, almost pushing me over. I made paper boats with Daddy's help, sailing them off into the swirling waves, and had fun imagining them landing on foreign shores. Mummy baked, and we had fresh warm bread and butter with whatever was in the larder for breakfast, lunch, and dinner. I played for a few days in that milky-tea river, making elaborate boats of all styles and sizes until the water finally receded.

I still hold a tableau vision of Mummy: she is wearing a blue gingham dress, a white belt around her waist, and white sandals on her bare feet. She is standing on the top step of the front porch. She looks happy, smiling, and waving to Daddy and me, standing in the middle of the rushing water. I'm in a baby blue seersucker swimsuit, and Daddy is wearing khaki shorts, a pale yellow, frayed, short-sleeved shirt, and green gumboots.

For those few days, while the road was impassable, Mummy went about her daily life: making bread, reading, crocheting, and writing letters. Daddy, unable to go down to the store for a drink, stayed home and built boats for me.

What was called "A terrible act of God" seemed like an incredible gift to me.

Life went as usual.
A president was assassinated.
Christmas came and went.
My periods started.

Lorna arrived from England shortly after Christmas. She brought with her two wool skirts and sweaters and a plum coloured coat with a huge black fur collar. Together, it weighed almost as much as I did. I didn't realise it at the time, but it was my wardrobe for the English winter.

On January 4th, I met a group of women dressed in white, Jehovah's Witnesses. They were declaring that the world would end in four days.

I was not prepared for the life changes that were about to happen. For me, their prediction came true. I would leave my island home, Mummy and Daddy, Bingo and Wong, on January 9th, 1964, and not return until December 1969.

An End of Innocence

I stood at the stern of a Van Geest banana boat, listening to the anchor clank, link by link, as a sailor turned the pulley, lifting it out of the water. I had a jumble of feelings. My heart and eyes focused on the tiny shape of the Citroën car as it wound its way up the coastal road from Kingstown, towards Cane Hill. Once, I thought I saw the car stop and I waved frantically, hoping Mummy and Daddy could see me. My eyes welled with tears as I tried hard to remember every detail of what they looked like as they stood on the dock, waving goodbye.

Mummy wore a yellow shirtwaist dress with lilac flowers. It came down to her calves. On her collar was her favourite brooch — folded ribbons of gold, loosely braided into two triangles with an emerald in the centre. Her slightly greying chestnut hair came to the middle of her back when she combed it out at night, but that day, it was rolled into a bun at the back of her head. She wore curved tortoiseshell combs above her ears to tame the fine flyaway ends that otherwise blew around her face. Her shoes were old white Clark sandals, which Daddy cleaned every day. The supple yellow rubber soles had long since worn off. Daddy had replaced them with hard leather. Inside her shoes, her feet were bare. The sandal's toe caps hid her fungus-gnarled toenails.

For the first time, I noticed a few wrinkles in the corners of Mummy's peaceful, blue eyes. Her face was soft and smooth. She wore no makeup and just a dab of Eau de Cologne; her smell fresh and comforting. The corners of her mouth had a slight upturn, but her Mona Lisa smile could become a tight line of disapproval in a second. She was my anchor, my mainstay, the thread that held my life together — until now.

Daddy was different. Although deep down I knew that he cared for me, he was unpredictable. Occasionally he was funny, but he was also dismissive of my feelings and often teased and made fun of me. He was also a chain-smoker, a cigarette usually hanging from his lips, his body permeated with the acrid, sickly smell of cheap tobacco.

When he worked in the fields, he protected his face and balding head, shiny red with perspiration, under a battered straw hat. Now, he wore khaki trousers to hide the gauze bandages he wrapped daily around his legs. They covered scaly red fungal patches, which he said was athlete's foot. At home, he wore shorts and long socks to cover the dressings. Each day, Daddy polished his brown leather shoes to a high shine. He told me he had learnt to "spit and polish" in the army. His round-frame glasses highlighted his bright, paler-than-the-sky, rimless blue eyes. They often danced with "mischief" or "evil merriment" (Mummy's words) when Daddy thought he had gained the advantage over a situation.

He also wore a clean Hawaiian cotton shirt, the wide scoop neck and armholes of his under-vest slightly visible through his shirt. He wore a jaunty new straw hat with a green ribbon on the side and a black binding around the edge. He smelled cool and fresh with his Limacol aftershave. I inhaled deeply as I kissed his cheek, hoping the lemony fragrance would last forever.

All the excitement since Lorna had arrived from England was gone now I knew I was going to be leaving my island home. I felt only a deep sense of fear painfully filling my body. There was anticipation, looking forward to an adventure, but fear, because it was unknown. I was fearful that I might never see Mummy and Daddy again.

I wanted to scream so loud that they would hear me and turn their car around. I felt like I wanted to jump overboard and swim home. Instead, I stood on the deck holding back my tears and fears. I told myself I was just being silly. Mummy wouldn't be pleased with my foolishness. Daddy might make some trivial remark that would hurt my feelings. I was only going for a year. Even I could manage that. I knew that they were old because the census, two years previous, had said, "beyond childbearing."

I felt that I must turn this time away into an adventure, then I would be back on my island in no time, and everyone would be excited to see me again. I would have wonderful and exciting stories to tell about England and France. Plus the final adventure: sailing back across the Atlantic with Lorna and Francis to St. Vincent.

It was January 9th, 1964. I was just over fourteen years old, small and immature for my age. I stood four feet nine inches tall and weighed only sixty-four pounds. The packing was simple. I had nothing of mine with me: no dolls, no books, no treasures, no pictures, not even my favourite teddy, his hair all worn off with years of use. Lorna considered him disgusting. I only had a box of 365 board games, which I received for my thirteenth birthday. I had told myself, I had my memories. I wouldn't need pictures or childish treasures. I was returning in a year.

I had a new trunk — at least, it was new to me. Daddy painted one of their old metal trunks a bright blue with my name, Jane Moller, in white, on the top. I put the clothes Lorna brought from England into it: two wool cardigans, one turquoise, and the other pink, both pretty but prickly to wear, and two straight skirts, one a muddy brown, the other blue. Both hung heavily on my waist and stopped my legs from moving comfortably; there'd be no jumping, running, or doing the splits in these skirts. I also had a coat. It was a rich overripe plum colour, with a large black fur collar, under which I felt I would buckle.

It had been fun trying on the clothes in our living room in Calliaqua. Mummy and Daddy laughed at my antics as I struggled with the strangeness of the clothes, especially a suspender belt (garter belt) and black stockings. I could not imagine why anyone would wear such an uncomfortable piece of clothing. Lorna left the room. She wasn't amused by my shenanigans. My new clothes once belonged to someone much older than me. According to Lorna, they were supposed to turn me into a "lady." Overnight, if she had her way!

No one would tell me why I was going to England. Mummy only said, "It's for the best." Daddy patted my head and told me to "run along and play." Lorna seemed to think I shouldn't be involved in any of the conversations. I heard whispered voices at night before I fell asleep. "You're both getting on in years. . . " "She's growing up. . . " "How will you. . ." "What if she's like. . . " none of it I understood.

I cried when Mummy told me a couple of nights before Lorna was due to leave that she was here to take me "home" to England, but there was no explanation of why I was going. Daddy didn't say anything when I kissed him goodnight or cuddled me on his lap. I never argued with adults, there was no point, none of them ever listened. I knew I could not change anyone's mind, certainly not Lorna's.

It took nine days for the Van Geest merchant ship to sail from Kingstown, St. Vincent, to Barry Docks in South Wales, England. I tried hard to make every day an adventure. There were only six passengers on board. Lorna and I, and two retired colonial couples. One couple was from Hong Kong. They were taking a tour of the Caribbean before returning to "good old Blighty," England. At the dinner table, one gentleman talked, in what I later discovered were called spoonerisms. I thought it was a strange word. He had never used any spoons! It did sound funny, but it was hard to follow what he was saying. The other couple was returning from India and English imperialism. The husband talked using only abbreviations, which I found confusing. I never did understand what he was talking about. The wives chatted with Lorna and occasionally smiled at me and said I was a "good girl."

Then, there were my alone times when I felt sad and lost. I'd crawl under the canvas and into the lifeboats; it was a great place to hide. No one ever found me there. I also sought out the highest spot I was allowed to go. I would sit there staring into the vast depths of the churning water. I'd think of being back on my island with Mummy and Daddy.

One place I did enjoy, was going to the bridge. I loved listening to the radio communication. It was there I met Ben. He was a young steward, near my age. He made me happy when I was feeling sad. We spent afternoons playing board games or touring the boat. Playing games was a welcome relief from the endless sea in all directions for days. He was my first love; he gave me my first grown-up kiss. I was surprised how it made my spine tingle from top to bottom and my insides do a somersault. It only happened once because Lorna saw us. She tried to make sure I never saw him again. Not even before disembarking.

I did not know that in three short months, my life would change dramatically. I would not spend the year with Lorna, nor go to school in France. I would never be the adventurer returning on the high seas to the admiration of all my school friends. Instead, I would move in with a family of six, none of whom I had known or seen before. The mother was Lorna's youngest sister, Thea. She had three children and a fourth soon to be born.

I found it very different living in a family with children. It was fun at times, but I missed Mummy and Daddy terribly, and still thought I would be returning home to St. Vincent. A few weeks after the baby was born, while sitting in the living room in front of the fire. Don, Thea's husband, suddenly said, "You know, Thea is your mother."

I was too stunned to say anything. I burst into tears. On rare occasions,

I wondered who my mother was. I thought it might be Anne or Lorna, but a daughter of Mummy's whom I had never seen or heard from before seemed impossible.

While I sobbed, Thea and Don seemed confused, unsure what to say or do. They did both say, "We don't want you to talk about what we have just told you, not even to the kids." I felt desperately alone and lost. I now had new parents whom I barely knew.

Nothing in my first fourteen years was as devastating as this. The trauma would fester as a loss of identity. Sleeping in the bed above one of my siblings, I sobbed myself quietly to sleep for many more nights. During the daytime, I strived to live without breaking down or telling my siblings that I was actually their half-sister. This helped me to accomplish school work and visits to Lorna and her husband, Francis. Inside, I was lost and hollowed out for a long time. I had no anchor. Mummy was thousands of miles away, and I wasn't able to tell her how I felt.

The cast and setting of my life suddenly changed. I was a teenager, the oldest of five children, and I was supposed to be responsible for them. For the next few years, I had no words to bridge the gap between the reality of my situation and how I had lived for my first fourteen years. I lived two lives: a secret, internal life of sadness and grief, and an outward life, crammed as full as possible with activities.

I did write home again, but not for a while. I began writing again after I received a short letter from Daddy. I left it unopened for days before reading it. Daddy never wrote letters. I thought something terrible had happened to Mummy. Fortunately, nothing unpleasant had happened. It was just a short note saying that they missed hearing my stories about school. It gave me the impetus to start writing again, but in secret. I always started, *Dearest Mummy and Daddy...*

For the next five years, I continued to live in England. I finished school, passed all my exams, had a few crushes on boys but never a boyfriend, until I met my future husband in my senior year. I was rarely at home. I put all my energy into being a Girl Guide Captain, working two jobs, and being with my boyfriend.

I moved out of the family house because of differing opinions. I moved in and out of several places of residence before I saved enough money to pay for my flight back to St. Vincent in December 1969 to see Mummy and Daddy again.

Anglican Church in Calliaqua

A centipede

The Cowbell

The white cross where Sylvester DeFreitas is buried

The diving board at the Aquatic Club

Mummy and Daddy, before Jane left St. Vincent

CPSIA information can be obtained
at www.ICGtesting.com
Printed in the USA
BVHW081418110922
646517BV00005B/35